"If you want to go quickly, go alone.
If you want to go far, go together."

—AFRICAN PROVERB

WHISTLE STOP
Café
MYSTERIES

Under the Apple Tree
As Time Goes By
We'll Meet Again
Till Then
I'll Be Seeing You
Fools Rush In
Let It Snow
Accentuate the Positive
For Sentimental Reasons
That's My Baby
A String of Pearls
Somewhere Over the Rainbow
Down Forget-Me-Not Lane
Set the World on Fire
When You Wish Upon a Star
Rumors Are Flying
Here We Go Again
Stairway to the Stars
Winter Weather
Wait Till the Sun Shines
Now You're in My Arms
Sooner or Later
Apple Blossom Time
My Dreams Are Getting Better

WHISTLE STOP
Café
MYSTERIES

MY DREAMS Are GETTING BETTER

JEANETTE HANSCOME

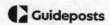

Guideposts

Whistle Stop Café Mysteries is a trademark of Guideposts.

Published by Guideposts
100 Reserve Road, Suite E200
Danbury, CT 06810
Guideposts.org

Cover and interior design by Müllerhaus
Cover illustration by Greg Copeland at Illustration Online LLC.
Typeset by Aptara, Inc.

ISBN 978-1-961441-93-4 (hardcover)
ISBN 978-1-961441-94-1 (epub)

Printed and bound in the United States of America
10 9 8 7 6 5 4 3 2 1

MY DREAMS Are GETTING BETTER

CHAPTER ONE

J anet Shaw hung a batter-splattered work apron on a hook in the Whistle Stop Café kitchen and studied her selection of 1940s-inspired smocks. As much as she could help it, flour and grease would not contaminate the darling aprons her mother had presented her with after church the previous afternoon.

"I found the patterns online." Mom had looked so proud when she handed Janet the tote bag. "I made five different ones for you, Debbie, and Paulette to share for the café's 'Throwback to 1945' countdown to Memorial Day."

An hour into the first Monday of May, cute aprons felt like the perfect addition to a month dedicated to honoring the eighty-year anniversary of Victory in Europe Day. Janet chose a blue-and-white gingham apron with a vintage image of a slice of cherry pie on one pocket and a frosted cupcake on the other. She grabbed two plates piled with breakfast goodness.

She nudged the double kitchen doors open with her hip and called for Debbie. "One stack of buckwheat pancakes with bacon and one calico scramble with wheat toast." She took a glance out the window to enjoy the morning sunlight. Only three days before, a freak May Day storm had soaked the area with torrential rain. Now, spring had settled in to stay.

Debbie swooped over from the cash register and whisked the plates from Janet's hands. "Thank you, ma'am. This will make some hungry customers very happy."

Janet tapped her foot to the rhythm of big band music playing over the sound system, compliments of the depot museum curator, Kim Smith's, extensive record collection. She admired the list of that day's throwback menu specials.

BREAKFAST – CALICO SCRAMBLE
(SCRAMBLED EGGS WITH BELL PEPPERS AND TOMATOES)
LUNCH – GRANDMA'S CHICKEN POT PIE
SOUP OF THE DAY – BEEF BARLEY
FROM THE HOMEFRONT BAKERY – VICTORY APPLE PIE

Scrumptious choices for the first full week of 1940s meals, baked goods, music, and red, white, and blue tablecloths.

After delivering the plates to a couple seated at a back corner table, Debbie returned to the area behind the counter. She stared at the specials board as if not quite satisfied. She plucked a piece of chalk off the tray at the bottom of the board and added a pretty flourish to each corner. "There we go."

Janet took time to appreciate her friend's lovely chalk swirls. "Now the board looks as cheerful as the rest of the café."

Debbie brushed dust off her hands, taking extra care, Janet noticed, with the wedding ring Greg Connor had placed on her finger only a couple of weeks before during their whirlwind wedding. "I heard news that my husband and the Dennison Event Planning Committee recruited Tiffany to oversee games for the Memorial

Day celebration." Her cheeks glowed a rosy shade of pink. "Is it weird that I love saying, 'my husband'?"

"No, I love hearing you say it." Janet was still getting used to thinking of her lifelong friend as a married woman. But she couldn't think of a better-suited couple than Debbie Albright and Greg Connor. "Tiffany is thrilled to be overseeing games. It'll keep her plenty busy until her lifeguard job starts the first week of June."

"When is your girl coming home for the summer?"

"Sunday." Tiffany had given her the final rundown of her schedule when they video chatted on Friday night. "She takes her last final on Thursday, plans to do absolutely nothing on Friday, will pack on Saturday, and is heading home Sunday to celebrate Mother's Day and start her game-planning extravaganza."

Extravaganza seemed like the ideal word for what the Chamber of Commerce Events Committee was advertising as A Memorial Day Celebration of the Decade. In a few weeks, the Dennison Depot would be the end point for a parade and the home to a community picnic complete with classic carnival games set up in railcars, and a snack bar that Janet's former Third Street Bakery boss, Charla Whipple, volunteered to run in the depot. Kim had just announced a half-price entry special for the Saturday before Memorial Day and created a Victory! exhibit dedicated to the end of World War II, open through the end of August.

Janet remembered a tray of peanut butter cookies that she still needed to add to the bakery case. "The Memorial Day event is going to be such a joyful lead-up to summer."

Debbie picked up a stack of freshly wiped-down menus. "To add to the excitement, I have renters confirmed for the rest of this month."

"That's right." Janet opened the case in preparation for adding the cookies. "You have those students from Case Western Reserve staying at your place." It was exciting to see Debbie build a new life with Greg while still holding on to the craftsman-style home she'd bought from Ray Zink by using it as a rental. For the next four weeks, Debbie would be hosting two graduate students from Case Western's premedical program who were doing a project on the secrets of longevity among those ninety and over. They'd chosen Good Shepherd Retirement Center as their first focus group. "I hope your students include Ray and Eileen." Ray would turn 100 in June and still had a twinkle in his eye. Especially when Eileen Palmer walked into the room. Eileen was the picture of health and joy at 102. Then there was Harry Franklin, who'd celebrated his ninety-seventh birthday on April 22 and still lived on his own. "Harry would be a great candidate too, even though he doesn't live at Good Shepherd."

Debbie set her stack of menus beside the cash register. "It wouldn't hurt to suggest him. I'm sure Jasmine and Amber will zero in on Ray and Eileen as soon as they walk into the retirement center. If anyone provides glowing examples of longevity, it's them."

Debbie went to the sink and filled a coffee carafe with water as she continued. "Jasmine and Amber are arriving tomorrow and plan to hit the ground running at Good Shepherd on Wednesday. The professor supervising their project has already paid the rent for May at my going rate."

"Lucky them. It sounds like their exam week ends early." Janet could still see Tiffany with no makeup on and her dark red hair in a ponytail, admitting to her typical pre-finals lack of sleep.

"Both mentioned having light course loads this semester while doing research." Debbie opened the top of the coffee maker and poured in the water.

Janet worked up the best impression of her mother from decades ago. "Have you met these students, so you know they aren't party animals?"

"Jasmine and Amber and I met via video call on Saturday night, and they are most definitely not party animals. More like some of the hardest workers I've ever spoken to. When they told me about their recent jobs and some of the courses they've taken, I felt like the biggest slacker of all time." Debbie reached under the counter for a bag of coffee. "They seem like great girls. Young women, I mean."

Janet started heading toward the kitchen for her cookies. "Anyone under thirty looks like a girl to me now that I'm nearing the tail end of my mid-forties. I still stock the cupboard with Tiffany's favorite cereal and junk food before she comes home for breaks."

Debbie plunged a scoop into the bag of coffee. "It's good to know I'm normal then. I took down a list of Jasmine's and Amber's favorite breakfast foods and snacks, even though I know they get a stipend for living expenses. They won't live on Ramen noodles on my watch."

"See, in a short time as a bonus mom of a fourteen-year-old and a sixteen-year-old, you already know the key to students' hearts. Snacks." Janet pushed one of the swinging doors.

"Except in Jasmine and Amber's case, the grocery bill will be less expensive. I'm learning why teenage boys are often referred to as bottomless pits."

The ding of the bell on the entrance triggered an instant turn of Janet's feet. At this time of morning, she always expected to see either Harry Franklin, his granddaughter, Patricia, or both. As predicted, Janet saw Harry at the door with his canine companion, Crosby. The cookies could wait. "Hello there, Harry."

"Morning, ladies." Harry did a nice little two-step. "I like the music."

Debbie drummed on the counter. "Isn't it great? We should have a dance party."

Greg Connor was right behind Harry with his sons, Jaxon and Julian.

Harry neared the counter. He thrust his thumb over his shoulder. "Look who I found wandering around aimlessly in the parking lot."

Kim Smith came through the door next. "What timing. I showed up when all the cool people are here." She made a beeline to the counter.

Janet evaluated the contents of her bakery case. If this parade of regulars was an indication of what she could expect today, she might run out of the good stuff by midmorning. "I'm not used to seeing you here on a Monday, Kim." The Dennison Depot Museum was usually closed on Mondays, but Kim looked ready for a busy day in casual slacks and a blue cardigan.

Harry led Crosby to a table. "Did you decide taking Mondays off was for wimps?"

"Not exactly." Kim shot Harry a smile then moved her gaze to the bakery selection. "My Victory exhibit opens tomorrow. I still have one more display to finish."

Debbie took a tray of clean cutlery off a cart beside the kitchen door and moved it to the back counter. "I can't wait to sneak over to see the whole exhibit."

Greg came around the counter to where Debbie stood with a handful of spoons and forks and gave her a peck on the cheek. "Hi, sweetheart."

"Aw." Kim grinned at Debbie. "You guys."

Jaxon shielded his brother's eyes. "Dad. There are children present."

Debbie patted Greg's face.

Janet couldn't recall when Debbie looked more radiant. "They have special permission to be mushy for at least another month." She made a mental note to finally give Debbie the cookbook she'd made as a wedding gift. All she needed to do was wrap it.

Julian let his backpack fall into a chair at the table beside him and took a turn showering Crosby with attention.

Debbie squeezed Greg's hand. "What can I get for you?"

"I'll have a large coffee." He turned to the boys. "Jaxon, Julian, do you know what you want?"

Janet playfully tapped the bakery counter. "What can I tempt you boys with this morning? A common, ordinary cinnamon roll or a vintage apple turnover fresh from the oven? I made some to use up crust from the victory apple pies."

Julian stood up from petting Crosby and went over to the case. "I can't decide. It all looks *so good*. I'm starving."

Greg's expression countered, *Are you kidding me?* "Didn't you just scarf down three eggs, a banana, two slices of toast, and a jumbo glass of milk?"

"I'm a growing boy." He settled on a turnover and orange juice. His brother ordered the same.

"So, young man." Harry gave Julian a friendly punch on the arm. "It's almost nine o'clock in the morning. Shouldn't you and your brother be at school by now?"

Crosby wandered over to Julian, dragging his leash with him.

"We have delayed starts today because of teacher meetings."

Jaxon joined his brother at the bakery case. "First period is at nine fifty for me and ten o'clock for Julian."

"We didn't have all those late starts and teacher workdays when I was a kid. Though I'm sure the teachers could've used a day off to work without us hooligans getting in their hair." Harry folded his arms across his chest. "I hear Julian's starting high school in the fall. Are you a genius yet?"

Julian wrinkled his nose and looked over at his dad. "I do okay."

"Yeah, I was a 'do okay' student too." Harry took a seat and slapped his knee for Crosby. He instantly ran over. "I could always count on an A in gym and history."

"I usually like PE." Julian sat with Harry. "But not this month."

Harry rubbed the space between Crosby's ears. "What's going on in PE that changed your mind?"

"Today we start a dancing unit. Ballroom and swing. *Ugh.*"

Janet got bags for the boys' turnovers. "I remember the dancing unit. Tiffany loved it."

Kim did a little jig with her feet. "In school I would've rather gotten a grade for dancing than my running or tennis skills. Or lack of."

Greg put his hands on his son's shoulders. "He's just upset because the class has to perform for the parents."

"On Friday night of Memorial Day weekend." Julian made a face like he'd just swallowed something nasty. "It will be graded, and we have to wear formal attire. That's what Mr. Blake called it. Attire."

Jaxon smacked his brother's back. "It's character building." He gruffed up his voice and expression to top off his grumpy old man impersonation. "I got through the dance unit and am a stronger person because of it."

Julian gave his brother the side-eye. "You tried to play sick the night of your performance."

Greg traced the seam of his cup with his fingers. "If I recall correctly, you pulled the old cliché faking a fever with a heating pad bit."

"I should've done better research. I gave myself a hundred and six temperature." He shook a finger at his brother. "But, in the end, I did the performance like a man."

Greg took two sugar packets from a basket on Harry's table. "Upon penalty of being grounded for the first week of summer break."

Debbie held three half-and-half cups out to her husband. "Well, I'm looking forward to the performance. It'll be my first school event as one of the parents."

"Here's a change of subject I think you'll all enjoy." Greg took a sip of his coffee. "How about if I let you be the first to hear a big announcement?"

Harry's eyes lit up. "Julian's class is going to lead the Memorial Day parade with a song-and-dance number?"

"Fortunately for Julian, the high school marching band is leading the parade."

Julian let out a loud sigh of relief.

"We need to cross our fingers that the band doesn't lose half its members to suspension for senior pranks."

Jaxon cut in, "Some seniors set off the fire alarm last week. They got in big trouble."

"What happened to moving the principal's car to the top of the science building or putting red dye in the swimming pool?" Debbie asked.

"Oh, hon." Greg patted her arm. "Those pranks are so two decades ago. Now for the announcement. The chamber of commerce met with our events committee over the weekend, and everyone agreed that something was missing from the Memorial Day parade. We have groups lined up to march and contribute the usual floats, but nothing exciting to set the parade apart from other years. So we are adding a float competition. The winner will get a trophy, and of course plenty of exposure in the *Gazette* and the local news. If the competition goes well, we might make it a regular thing and pass the trophy on to each new winner."

Julian smoothed down his hair. "That sounds cool."

"Can anyone enter a float?" Jaxon asked.

"Yep. Groups just need to register so we know how many to plan for." Greg peeled back the cover of a half-and-half cup. "I wrote an announcement for local businesses and clubs that will go out this morning. I'm planning to enter a float for Connor Construction. We're hoping to get all age groups involved." He poured in his half-and-half and opened another. "A list of requirements should go up on the chamber of commerce event website before noon. For now, I can tell you the floats need to reflect either the end of World War II, memorialize some who died, or honor those who contributed to the war effort."

Debbie leaned against the back counter. "The time frame seems tight. The parade is only four weeks away."

"That came up." Greg went over to the trash can beside the counter and tossed in his empty cups. "So we're making it part of the judging criteria—who can come up with something creative in a short time."

Janet glanced over at Debbie. "We should enter one for the café." A possibility started taking shape in her mind.

Kim stuffed some napkins into her turnover bag. "I wish I could enter a float for the museum, but I'm already swamped with the Victory exhibit. I have school groups booked all month long."

"Maybe I can draft you to announce the winner?"

"Count me in." Kim put her pastry bag into her tote. "I can't wait to see what everyone comes up with."

Janet bagged two more plump apple turnovers for the boys. She handed them across the counter to Jaxon and made a run to the kitchen for containers of juice.

Once everyone had what they'd ordered, Janet remembered the tray of peanut butter cookies and a victory apple pie cooling in the kitchen. "I better get the rest of my goodies out before the breakfast rush really takes off." She hurried to the kitchen. While transferring the cookies from the cooling rack to a bakery tray, she pictured herself and Debbie doing delicate queen waves from the top of a float, their hair in victory curls.

When she returned with the cookies, Julian was wedging his juice into the water bottle slot of his backpack. "I can tell you one thing. My float won't include dancing of any kind." He nudged Harry. "But yours could."

Harry stared up at the ceiling then down at Crosby, who was looking up at his owner as if he had a great idea of his own. "Nah, I have something else in mind."

Jaxon unscrewed the cap of his orange juice bottle. "You know what you're doing already?"

"Sure do." Harry opened his menu. "It'll feel good to do this again."

Janet set her tray of cookies on top of the bakery case. "You've entered a float competition before? We learn something new about you every day, Harry."

"It wasn't a competition, just a celebration. In 1946, Dennison marked the one-year anniversary of World War II ending with a parade and community picnic. Eileen asked for my help with a float for the depot. The chamber of commerce couldn't have afforded a trophy back then even if they wanted to make it a contest. It was all about celebrating and being together."

Julian took his turnover out of the bag. "What are you going to do for your float, Mr. Franklin?"

Harry picked up his menu and shook his head. "Can't tell you. You might steal my idea."

"I would never."

"I'm just messin' with you. But my float idea is still a secret." Harry shut his menu with a smack. "I can't get too excited about it anyway. The whole thing coming together as I'm picturing depends on me finding something that I haven't seen in quite a while."

Janet watched Harry's expression. What could he possibly have in mind?

CHAPTER TWO

Harry Franklin parked his luggage cart in the back corner of the quiet waiting area. The depot entrance opened, letting in a beam of May sunshine and his girlfriend, Sylvia McCurdy. Harry waved to her then straightened the cart.

Part of him still pictured Sylvia as she looked on the day they met in April 1945, wearing a railroad mechanic's uniform, her coiled black hair pulled up in a scarf, proudly holding a toolbox.

Other times, he imagined her on May 8 of that same year, when Miss Eileen came running out of the depot, tears streaming down her face, shouting, "Harry, Sylvia, the war in Europe is over," and Sylvia threw her arms around Harry's neck. In the celebratory flurry of hugs and cheers and tears of relief that brought work at the depot to a halt, Harry had swooped Sylvia up. Their lips met for the first time. He still didn't know who kissed who first that day. It didn't matter. She'd been his girl ever since.

On this late Saturday afternoon, Sylvia wore ordinary weekend clothes—jeans, blue sneakers with white soles, a red checked blouse—and her hair pulled back with a matching band. How he had ended up with the prettiest girl in Dennison, Harry would never know.

She ran over to him. "I hope I'm not late." Sylvia's smile lit up the depot and Harry's heart. "Mama and I have been spring cleaning all day. I wanted to freshen up."

"You're not late." Harry checked the luggage cart to make sure the wheels weren't cockeyed. "I just finished my end-of-shift work. Miss Eileen said she'd be out in a minute."

Sylvia took a seat on the bench closest to her. She stretched out her legs and crossed one foot over the other. "Do you know what she wants to talk to us about?"

"Not even a hint." All he knew was Miss Eileen seemed excited when she asked to meet with him and Sylvia, so it couldn't be bad news.

Harry saw his fellow porter, Mitch Macomb, come out of the area where station employees clocked in and out. Mitch gave a half salute, half wave. Harry left Sylvia to go clock out. When he returned, Eileen Turner, the stationmaster, was in the waiting area with Sylvia.

Miss Eileen rested her hand on the back of the bench. "So, Sylvia, you and Harry are graduating high school next month, and you with straight A's, I hear. Do you have any big plans yet?"

"Nothing too exciting, I'm afraid. College isn't something my parents can afford right now, so I'm looking for a job. No leads yet." She motioned Harry over and patted the place beside her. "It'll be hard to find something that compares to working as a mechanic with my aunt Marion during the war. I feel a little guilty for missing it, knowing I gave it up because all the men in my family came home from the war safe. My uncle even found mechanic jobs for my father and brother."

"You're not alone, Sylvia," Miss Eileen said. "Lots of women have found it difficult to adjust to life at home after working in the factories and shipyards."

Harry took a seat beside Sylvia. "I'm glad your father and brother got those positions. It meant you got to stay in Dennison instead of moving back to Columbus." When he met Sylvia, she and her mother were only in Dennison temporarily, staying with her aunt Marion to share expenses. Now Sylvia's family lived in their own home.

"That's another thing I remind myself of." She gave Harry a cute little wink. "I just never expected to enjoy working with my hands so much. Dad asks me for help with repairs around the house as often as he asks my brother."

Miss Elieen found a place on the bench on the other side of Sylvia. "I have something to keep you busy after school and on weekends. You too, Harry."

Harry watched Sylvia's face brighten over the mention of a project.

Miss Eileen shifted her feet as if she wished she could kick off her shoes but knew it would be unprofessional. "I'm sure you both heard about the Memorial Day Honor Parade and Community Picnic."

The one-year anniversary celebration of the end of the war had been the talk of Dennison since before Easter. "My parents were just talking about it last night," Harry told Miss Eileen. It would include a bake sale and raffle to support the VA, a veterans' parade, and music. Harry had heard talk around town that the chamber of commerce planned to thank locals who contributed to the war effort and give a special honor to the Salvation Army for their canteen.

The canteen had closed two weeks ago, after the last troop train stopped transporting soldiers home. It still felt strange to no longer have the Salvation Army ladies and their volunteers at the station with long tables of sandwiches, cookies, chewing gum, and magazines, the lines of men in uniform receiving free sack lunches and anything else they wanted for the next leg of the journey. Harry even missed seeing the silly behavior of some of the girls who liked to flirt with the men going off to fight. But the absence of the canteen meant the end of a long war that took the lives of far too many of those soldiers.

Sylvia shifted around and tucked one leg under the other. "Some ladies at church are making pies for the bake sale. My mother and aunt are both on the committee. They're already arguing over who makes the best apple crumble."

Miss Eileen's blue eyes twinkled. "If anyone from the event planning committee overheard that debate, they might add a baking contest to the festivities. Instead, they've asked groups that played a part in the war effort to contribute floats for the veterans' parade. Fletcher Memorial Hospital is creating one, along with the Salvation Army, the Red Cross, the Women's Auxiliary, the VA, and our very own depot." She leaned her elbow on the bench back. "I think it's a wonderful idea, but I don't know how I'll manage to design a float with all I have to do as stationmaster. Would the two of you be willing to lend your creativity to our float committee?"

Sylvia didn't pause for even a moment. "I would love to help you out, Miss Eileen. I'm sure my parents will approve. Mama teased me today that sometimes I get so restless that she wants to shoo me outdoors to play. I'll start thinking of some ideas for designs that will honor the day."

Harry couldn't imagine Miss Eileen finding the time to work on a float between her responsibilities at the station and supporting her father, who'd been wounded in the First World War. "You don't have to worry about a thing, Miss Eileen. I'm not quite as handy with tools and creative ideas as Sylvia is, but I can certainly manage a hammer and paint roller."

"That's what I was hoping for. I will help as much as I can. But I have a feeling you'll come up with a much more festive design than I could on my own. Something like this needs a youthful touch."

On the walk home from the depot, Harry took Sylvia's hand as they made their way down Main Street. "Do you want to stop at the drugstore for a pop before heading home? My treat." He figured she'd earned it after spending her Saturday on spring cleaning.

"I'd like that. Thanks."

Harry tightened his hold on Sylvia's hand and made a beeline for the drugstore. "A pop sounds refreshing right now."

A tapping noise on the sidewalk drew Harry's attention away from anticipating the flavor of a cold, fizzy drink. A familiar young man walked toward them on the sidewalk, moving a white cane to one side then the other. Harry stepped back to get out of his way. Sylvia followed suit.

He knew the man well. It was Mitch's older brother, Bradley. Before joining the army, Bradley had worked as a ticket seller at the depot. Now, he was one of many young men who'd come home from battle with an injury that changed his life forever.

Harry struggled to untie his tongue. Just say hi.

"Hello, Bradley." Sylvia addressed him without a bit of the uneasiness Harry felt. "It's Sylvia McCurdy."

"And Harry Franklin," Harry added. He tried to chase away the tension in his gut, the feeling of not knowing what to say to a twenty-year-old who could see when he joined the army in the summer of 1944 and couldn't when he returned to Dennison less than a year later.

Bradley stopped and poised his cane so it stood straight up in his right hand like a shepherd's staff. "Afternoon, Sylvia. Hi, Harry."

"How are you doing today?" Sylvia asked him.

"I'm well, thanks. Just out for a walk."

Harry looked into Bradley's blue eyes. If he didn't know one eye was glass and the other no longer saw clearly, both irreparably damaged by shrapnel, he never would have guessed. Bradley had been blinded during the battle of Okinawa, just a month after being shipped off to Japan. According to what Mitch had shared with Harry, Bradley could see shadows and shapes with his "good eye" as he put it, but not nearly enough to make up for the lack of his other eye. He couldn't read print in books or newspapers anymore. Faces were blurry and he constantly fought eye strain, even when looking at his pretty girlfriend, Margo.

Harry tried to imagine what it would be like to wake up in a military hospital knowing he'd never see Sylvia's smile clearly again. To spend weeks in a convalescent hospital learning to navigate the world without sight, and to know getting around safely in the town he'd lived in since birth would require using a white cane. Bradley had lost his sight at almost nineteen, only a few months older than Harry was now.

"It's a nice day for walking." Sylvia smiled directly at Bradley as if nothing about him had changed.

"Sure is. A nice day to get out and practice with this thing." He tapped his cane on the sidewalk.

"You're getting around well." Harry remembered the first time he saw Bradley walking alone down Main Street. He'd missed the curb and tripped. The lady who owned the fabric store rushed over to help him up, only to have Bradley insist, "I'm under strict orders to pick myself up when I trip." His shamed expression, like he wanted to escape much faster than his mobility allowed, stuck with Harry.

"You should've seen me when I had to take a walk around the hospital alone for the first time. I almost started crying like a baby." When Bradley laughed, he almost sounded like the Bradley who used to joke around with Harry and Mitch at the depot. But there was a catch in his voice. "Before I left the hospital, my aide advised me to get out as much as possible so I wouldn't lose my nerve."

"You've taken that seriously." I would never want to leave my house.

"It beats feeling sorry for myself. I did enough of that after my eye surgery. I'm on my way to meet Margo at the hospital so I can walk her home from work."

"We better let you go then," Sylvia insisted. "So you won't be late."

"Yeah, I'm surprising her." Bradley extended his cane in front of him. He pointed his index finger straight head, to the right, then straight again, whispering directions under his breath, his eyes fixed in concentration. Then he smiled and waved. "Off I go."

Harry waved back out of habit.

Sylvia called to him, "Say hello to Margo for us."

"I will."

Harry waited until he and Sylvia reached the drugstore to say what was on his mind. "I never know what to say to Bradley. I end up feeling clumsy and saying things that sound dumb." He paused at the door. "I feel bad for him."

"Say what you would've said to him before the war. When I catch myself feeling nervous around one of the wounded men, I tell myself, 'He's the same person. No one likes being treated differently because of a disability.'"

"That's a good thing to keep in mind." Harry held the door open for Sylvia. He followed her inside.

"But I do understand you feeling bad for him." Sylvia stopped in front of a big icebox with CHILLED POP printed across the front in fancy red letters. "Bradley was an artist, you know. Before the war. I saw him in a group picture in the art room at school, from a competition where he won first place in the sculpting category. A girl from our school took second."

"I forgot about Bradley being an artist." Harry stared at the sign on the front of the icebox with each pop flavor printed on a circle made to look like a bottle cap. Grape, root beer, strawberry, cola, cherry cola. Bradley couldn't even choose his own pop flavor without help. He probably felt like a little kid again half the time. "What flavor would you like?"

"Cherry cola, please." Sylvia folded her arms against the chill of the drugstore. "I was just thinking, Harry. Bradley must have a lot of time on his hands. What would you say about us inviting him to help with the float? Once we run the idea past Miss Eileen, of course."

Harry opened the icebox and found one last bottle of cherry cola poking through the ice cubes. "Do you think he'd be able to manage? I mean, he can't—"

"He can see a little bit. And his artistic mind still works fine, I'm sure." Sylvia brushed a bit of ice off her bottle. "It wouldn't hurt to ask. Even if he says no, he might appreciate being invited."

Harry pictured Bradley walking alone down the sidewalk while his younger brother worked at the station like always, not much to do but practice getting *around Dennison and walk Margo home from her nursing job. Whenever he saw Bradley, he was either alone, with Margo, or with his brother or parents. Never with his old friends from high school who'd returned from the war. "That's a nice idea." He chose a chilled bottle of root beer for himself. "If he's as artistic as you say, he might be able to help us come up with some good ideas."*

Sylvia led the way to the counter. "He might surprise you and take charge of the whole operation."

Harry set down two nickels and said hello as the cashier removed their bottle caps with an opener. He said thank you, handed Sylvia her drink, and held the door open for her. "Whether Bradley takes charge or not, I like the idea of getting him involved." By the time he took his first sip of root beer he didn't only want Bradley involved, he found himself praying for God to help them come up with something special for Bradley to do. Something that put his artistic skills on display for the whole town.

CHAPTER THREE

*J*anet scooped a ladleful of chili from the pan on the stove into a container. Her husband, Ian, reached around her for the plastic wrap and covered the round pan of remaining corn bread from their Monday night dinner.

With summer on its way, chili and corn bread season was about over. But now that Janet needed to add designing and decorating a float to her schedule, she'd pulled out some favorite one-pot meals that would provide tasty leftovers. "We can have chili on baked potatoes tomorrow night. Debbie, Paulette, and I have a float planning meeting after the café closes."

Ian put the plastic wrap back in its drawer. "You aren't wasting any time getting a float together."

"Not at all." Janet snapped a lid onto the container and found a place for it in the refrigerator. "I'm going to be dreaming about floats from now until the end of May. Homecoming floats. Me trying to serve food from a float."

Ian pushed the covered corn bread pan to the back of the counter. "You on a float as the Homecoming Queen."

"Ha!" Janet shut the fridge. "That's very sweet of you."

"The department isn't wasting time either. Floats were the theme of the day as soon as Greg's notice came through."

"Ooh, a little friendly competition."

"Who said anything about friendly?"

Janet opened the dishwasher. She tried to predict what the Dennison Police Department might come up with. "Are you going to enter a paddy wagon?"

Ian scraped chili residue from a bowl into the garbage disposal. He gave the bowl a good swoosh with the sponge. "We're more creative than that."

"But I bet it came up as a suggestion during your first brainstorming session."

"Okay, yes, it did. But it took about two seconds for us to agree a paddy wagon doesn't have anything to do with World War II or Memorial Day."

"Too bad. All joking aside, a paddy wagon would be cute."

"It would be. If Tiffany weren't in charge of games, we could've recruited her as one of the suspicious characters we rounded up."

"You would've locked up your own daughter?"

"For a chance at a trophy, absolutely."

Janet imagined Tiffany with her red hair teased and wild. "Come to think of it, Tiffany would be all for it."

"Instead, we're doing a tribute to the Military Police Corps."

"That's a wonderful idea. People don't often think of them when they talk about the war." Janet took Ian's bowl from him and put it in the dishwasher then added her own. All the talk about float plans made her even more enthused about the planning session with Debbie and Paulette. The idea she'd had when Greg announced the contest was getting more vivid by the hour. "Debbie was going to call me tonight with a meeting time for tomorrow. Let me check my messages, then we can relax for the evening. I need to wrap Debbie's cookbook, but I'll do that in the living room while we watch something on TV. You can be my assistant."

When Janet dug her phone out of her tote bag in the entry hall, she found two voice messages, one from Debbie and another from a friend she hadn't seen or heard from since before the café opened.

Mandy Hermon.

Seeing Mandy's name on her home screen stirred fond memories of hanging out in the student union at Cleveland State University. She and Mandy met as sophomores and graduated in the same year as Applied Food Science majors. While going in their own directions after college, they'd kept in touch as much as college friends could when they lived in different parts of Ohio. Mandy had married her husband, Gary, the same year Janet married Ian. She had twin daughters a year before Tiffany came along and raised them in Cincinnati. Whenever Janet and Ian were traveling that way, or vice versa, they made a point to get together. Until three years ago, barely a month after Janet, Ian, and Tiffany stopped in on Mandy's family during a road trip to Cuyahoga Valley National Park, when Gary passed away from a massive heart attack. Mandy's usual photo Christmas cards stopped. Janet had called and texted to check in whenever Mandy came to mind, but she'd only received short responses. She'd taken the cue that her grieving friend needed space.

Janet felt as eager to hear Mandy's voice as Debbie's update on where to meet and when.

Janet listened to Debbie's message, added *Float planning— Debbie's house* to her phone calendar for the next day at three o'clock, then played the other voicemail.

"Hi, Janet. This is Mandy Hermon. I know it's been a long time." Mandy sounded as sprightly as during their college years. "I'm in your area for a while and would love to meet for coffee. Give me a call when you get a chance."

Janet saw that Ian had already moved to the living room and went in to show him Mandy's name in her message box. "I'm going to return her call, then I'll join you."

Janet hit the callback button.

Mandy picked up halfway through the first ring. "Hi, stranger."

"Hello, yourself. It's nice to hear your voice."

"It's good to hear yours." The clanking in the background gave away that Mandy must be cooking something. In college, she became famous for her ability to turn cheap starving student fare into delicious creations.

Janet went to the kitchen so Ian wouldn't have to listen to half a phone conversation. "How've you been?"

"Okay. The last few years have been an adjustment, but I feel like I'm finally getting on track. We have a lot to catch up on, I know."

"Did I hear you say you're in the area?"

"You did. I'm teaching a class in Barnhill. I can't wait to tell you about it. My sessions are from eight to ten in the morning and one thirty to three thirty in the afternoon. Other than that I'm free. Do you have time for coffee or lunch sometime this week?"

"Sure. I co-own a café now, with my friend Debbie, but we close at two."

"Do you want to get coffee after one of my afternoon classes?"

Janet thought about her commitment to the parade. They should probably work it in before float construction consumed her schedule. "Are you free Thursday?"

"How about four o'clock? I'm staying at a bed and breakfast in Uhrichsville and saw a coffee shop this morning called Totally Awesome Coffee. I haven't tried it, so I can't vouch for the quality, but I can't resist the name."

"I know that place." They'd only been open for a few months but had already earned a reputation for their '80s vibe and unique coffee drinks. "I haven't tried it either but have wanted to. All their menu items include a reference to '80s pop culture."

"I wondered when I saw *totally awesome*. I'll meet you there."

"I look forward to catching up." She ended the call and joined Ian in the living room. She found him flipping through television channels.

"How's Mandy doing?"

"She sounds great. And extremely eager to meet."

Early the next morning, Janet stared into a mixing bowl. She'd just filled her rectangular pan and put it in the oven, yet the bowl still contained the equivalent of another cake. "How did this happen?" She ran her finger along the edge of the bowl and tasted a bit of the batter to make sure she hadn't destroyed that day's Homefront Bakery special by adding too much of something. She rechecked her recipe and discovered that while mentally planning a possible float design, her excitement over presenting Debbie with her cook-book, and speculating about Mandy Hermon's reappearance, she'd doubled it.

Debbie came through the kitchen doors and hung up her jacket. "I call dibs on the pink granny-style apron with the daisies and heart-shaped pockets."

"It's yours."

"Jaxon said seniors pulled another prank today. It wasn't serious enough to warrant punishment. Just sticky notes instructing fresh-men to do silly things like 'Bow to the next senior you see.'"

"The seniors are on fire this year."

"They got a warning to stop the pranks for the year. Hey, I smell carrot cake."

Janet tipped her bowl of batter. "What do you think about us occasionally offering samples of our throwback bakery specials, as an extra something fun? We could start today."

"Sure. Go for it." Debbie put the apron over her head. The dai-sies and heart pockets brought out her springtime newlywed glow. "This month is all about celebrating."

"I was hoping you'd say that." Janet presented the leftover carrot cake batter. "I'll serve them in the cupcake wrappers from Easter." She put it aside and sneaked over to where she'd left her tote bag. "That apron looks adorable on you, by the way."

"Thank you. You can tell your mom that yesterday three cus-tomers asked me where I bought my apron." She put her hands in the heart pockets and struck a sideways pose.

"She will consider that the highest compliment." Seeing Debbie in her cute apron made Janet feel frumpy in the boring one she'd been baking in since the wee hours, and she wanted to look her best when giving Debbie's gift. "Could you hand me the apron with the cherries on it?" It reminded her of a sundress she'd had as a little girl.

Debbie tossed it to her.

Janet did a quick apron change before hiding the present behind her back. "I have a little something for you. It's a wedding gift."

"You didn't have to get me a wedding present."

"Technically, I made it."

Debbie smiled and set the package on a clean area of the counter. She tugged one end of the poofy white bow Janet had created with Ian.

"I went a little nuts with the bow size. That's how excited I was to finally give this to you."

"I love the bow." Debbie laid it aside and peeled the tape without tearing the wrapping. She let the paper fall onto the floor. "Janet. You wrote this?" Debbie opened the cover and started flipping through the pages.

"It was my secret project. I took some of those photos right under your nose."

"My friend the stealth photographer." Debbie threw her arms around Janet. "I will treasure it." She held the cookbook to her heart. "Maybe we can sell copies in the café."

"I had been thinking about that. But more than anything, it's a thank-you for making me your partner at the café."

"I couldn't dream of a better partner."

Janet watched Debbie stash the cookbook in her bag and take it out again for another perusal. She allowed herself a moment to relive the fun of gathering all the recipes, snapping the photos, and watching her vision become even better than she'd expected.

"I can't wait to try one of these recipes out on Greg and the boys." Debbie gathered the wrapping and ribbon and tucked them into her tote. "Greg had a bright idea for his Connor Construction float last night. He thought it would be fun to reenact the famous end-of-the-war photo of a sailor dipping his girlfriend and kissing her in New York City."

"Now there's an injury waiting to happen."

"That's what I told him. I also reminded him I'm needed for the café float."

"That's right. He may be the love of your life, but Paulette and I need you more."

"Can you imagine Greg leaning me backward for the entire parade? Or to even repeat the dip over and over again. If we didn't both pull a vital muscle, I'd end up on my rump the first time we hit a bump in the road."

Janet poured a little vegetable oil in her baking pan to grease it. "Poor Greg. His first creative idea as a married man got shot down."

"I did it gently." Debbie went to the storage cupboard and came back with the Easter cupcake wrappers. "He came up with a Plan B. While Greg's grandfather was fighting in Europe, his grandma started a neighborhood victory garden and taught some of the other women how to can. When her husband was killed, the activities kept her going. She left a bunch of old posters behind. They have slogans like *Can all you can*, and *Grow your own, Can your own*. So Greg's going to pay tribute to her contribution and work in a way to honor his grandpa at the same time."

"Decorating should be a breeze. All Greg needs to do is have the boys dump potting mix into the back of his truck then stick in some tomato plants."

"That's what I said. Easy peasy. I'll have a ready-made vegetable garden."

"Exactly."

By the time Patricia Franklin came into the café for her traditional peppermint mocha, Janet had her first carrot cake frosted, a neat row of slices in the bakery case, and some samples created from corner pieces. Patricia sat herself down at the counter, dressed in a lovely sky-blue top that looked stunning against her dusky skin.

Janet snapped the tongs. "What can I get for you today?"

"Hmm." Patricia tucked her purse under her stool and stared up at the specials board. "Too bad it's a little early for carrot cake." She smacked the surface of the counter. "Wait. It's never too early for carrots."

"I agree."

Patricia licked her lips. "Carrot cake it is."

While Debbie started preparing the mocha, Janet found a middle piece with lots of frosting and set it in front of Patricia.

"Right behind you with a steaming hot peppermint mocha." Debbie edged her way behind Janet with Patricia's drink.

"What service." Patricia took her fork in one hand and a napkin in the other. "I don't know if my GP would approve of my daily sugar fest, but it sure gets my day started on a happy note." She shook her napkin out just as the welcome bell rang on the entrance. "See what I mean. Even the napkins are singing this morning."

Kyle Eger, who owned Eger's Market & Deli on Third Street, approached the counter with his thirteen-year-old son, Tristan, a few paces behind him. A rush of sadness swept over Janet. Seeing Kyle in the café on a weekday morning drove home the sad reminder that Eger's Market & Deli had been closed since the May 1st storm caused a partial roof collapse. Thankfully, the collapse happened in the middle of the night when the store was empty.

She'd heard rumors of Eger's closing for good because of it but refused to believe them. Eger's had been open for only a few years. Kyle and his wife, Renee, moved to Dennison from Portland, Oregon, to buy his grandfather's convenience store and update it for a twenty-first century clientele. They'd brought their foodie influence with them from the West Coast, providing scrumptious sandwiches, salads that went beyond the typical potato, macaroni, or coleslaw, and a great selection of gourmet dips, spreads, cheeses, and chips.

Janet's mouth watered just thinking about her last chicken salad on sourdough with a side of pesto and olive pasta from Eger's, the Sunday before the big rain event.

Kyle's droopy expression kicked in Janet's instinct to show care through treats. She rushed to the kitchen and returned with her tray of carrot cake samples. "Good morning. Can I interest you in a taste of today's bakery special? Carrot cake was popular during the war because carrots and spices are naturally sweet. I cheated and added cream cheese frosting." She'd read enough wartime recipes to know sugar, butter, and cream cheese would have been saved for company and holidays in the average home. She'd even read that icing on cakes was banned in Britian during the war as frivolous and wasteful. But even during a month of historical recipes, the thought of offering bare carrot cake was more than she could handle.

Kyle reached for a sample. "I'll give it a try."

Tristan shook his head. "I don't like cream cheese."

His father gave him a look.

"I mean, no thanks. I'm not fond of cream cheese."

Tristan's face bore a moody teen sulk. Janet had never dealt with a middle school-aged boy of her own, but she vividly remembered the roller coaster of ushering a girl through those years. Tristan had more than the anguish of his eighth-grade existence to make him grumpy. Based on Kyle's demeanor, Janet guessed life in the Eger home had to be stressful right now.

Kyle appeared downright depressed, wearing an Oregon State sweatshirt, his hair covered with a baseball cap, and a five-o'clock shadow at eight a.m. Before the cave-in, Kyle often stopped by the café midmorning for coffee, always clean shaven and professional and ready with news of a deli special to tempt Janet and Debbie. The last time Janet saw Kyle's wife, Renee, in passing after church, her eyes looked red from crying.

Janet took a step back to let Kyle and Tristan decide what they wanted.

Paticia got up to take another napkin from the dispenser at the end of the counter. "How are repairs on the store coming along, Kyle?"

Kyle glanced over at his son in a way that told Janet repairs were a sore subject. "We're dealing with the insurance company right now."

Patricia took her wad of napkins back to her place. "That's never fun."

"Not at all, I'm afraid."

Patricia gave Tristan a warm look, like she wanted to give him a big hug or a treat. "Tristan, are you getting excited about the end of middle school?"

He shrugged. "I guess."

"Are you involved in the parade at all?"

Tristan's eyes suddenly perked up a little. "Are we going to be, Dad? Yesterday during math, I heard Julian Connor talking about a float competition."

Kyle pulled out his wallet. "I got an email about that yesterday."

"Are you and Mom entering a float for the store?"

Janet watched the hope in Tristan's face intensify.

"I don't think so." Kyle ordered a large coffee.

"Why not?"

"Because it's pointless when—" Kyle adjusted his cap and shifted his eyes away from Tristan. "The store isn't open right now. Your mom and I don't have time for projects like that anyway. Sorry, Tris."

Janet couldn't decide who she felt worse for. Tristan or Kyle.

Patricia went back to sipping her mocha. Her strained face cried out to Janet, *I think I caused a problem.*

Tristan seemed oblivious to the audience around him. "But it might bring in some business."

"Tris, there's a hole in the roof."

Tristan shoved his hands into the pockets of his hoodie and mumbled, "There won't be a hole forever."

"How about if you tell Mrs. Shaw what you want from the bakery? You don't want to be late for school."

Tristan's expression fell again. "I'll have a cinnamon roll and a milk." He took a step back. "Please."

"Coming right up."

Patricia leaned her head toward Tristan. "If it makes you feel any better, I'm not entering a float either. I can't come up with a connection between my law practice and World War II. I'm bummed."

"At least I'm not the only one."

Debbie filled a large to-go cup with fresh coffee. "What can I get you to go with your coffee, Kyle?"

Janet waited for Kyle to go into his typical routine of saying, "This is supposed to be the year I lay off sweets," eyeing his son's cinnamon roll, then caving and ordering one for himself.

"No thanks." Kyle didn't even give the bakery case a sideways glance. "Just the coffee." He took a twenty-dollar bill out of his wallet and made his way over to the register. "There's a lot of buzz about the float competition."

Debbie took Kyle's cash. "It'll be interesting to see what people come up with in a short amount of time."

Janet couldn't take her eyes off Tristan. His disappointment over not entering a float was palpable. Before she could catch her own words, a thought flew from her brain and out of her mouth. "You know, Kyle, Tristan has a good point about a float bringing in business. Seeing the Eger's name will remind the community that you aren't going anywhere. You could hand out coupons with a QR code for special discounts. You know, for when you open again." She exchanged looks with Patricia. *I think I caused a problem too.*

Tristan sent his dad a pleading gaze. "I know how to make a QR code. It takes like five minutes."

Janet placed Tristan's sticky cinnamon roll in a to-go box and slid it across the counter to him, then made a dash to the kitchen for a small container of milk. She handed it over to Tristan then went over to Kyle's side of the counter. "Sorry for inserting my unsolicited idea."

"No worries. Your point is a good one." Kyle looked over to his son. "Tell you what. We can talk to your mom about it, and if she's on board we'll give it a try."

"Cool!"

He ushered his son toward the exit. "But you'll need to help with the whole process and come up with something that doesn't cost a fortune."

"I think I already have an idea."

The door shut before Janet could hear Tristan bounce his idea off Kyle, but through the window she noted the spring in Tristan's step. She watched him gesture with his free hand. She drew Debbie over before the father/son duo disappeared. "He looks like he's trying to talk his dad into a puppy. 'I'll feed him and walk him and bathe him and pay for his shots, I promise.'"

Debbie laughed out loud. "The competition is growing every day."

Patricia picked up a forkful of carrot cake. "I hope Kyle enters the contest. Every bit of business will help the store once they reopen. And doing something related to their market will give them hope."

Debbie went back to the coffee station. "It's clear by looking at Kyle and Tristan that they could use a big dose of that."

Janet was about to head to the kitchen when Patricia started up a conversation with Debbie.

"How's life as a married woman?"

"I know this might sound corny, but it's like a dream. I keep waiting for one of those 'The honeymoon is over' moments, but it hasn't happened yet."

"So, what's your favorite thing to do as a couple?"

Debbie reached into a box of half-and-half cups and pulled out a fistful. "Considering that we both own a business, we're happy to have time together. Last night, for example, Greg and I spent a very romantic evening getting my old house prepped for Jasmine and Amber to arrive today. It's all ready with fresh sheets on the beds, food in the fridge, and a welcome basket of pampering products on the dining room table."

"I want to rent your house."

Janet started toward the kitchen. This lull wouldn't last forever. "If the float competition becomes a regular thing and word gets around about it, tourists will have another reason to visit Dennison. They'll need places to stay. I predict Debbie's house will be the most popular rental."

A few minutes before noon, Janet bobbed her head to the beat of Les Brown's Orchestra and a young Doris Day singing "My Dreams Are Getting Better All the Time." Based on her experience from the day before, she expected the lyrics to create an earworm into the evening, until tomorrow's playlist provided another one. She didn't care a bit. The lyrics were just corny enough to be charming. Janet poked American flag toothpicks into two meat loaf lunch specials and danced the plates out the Debbie, singing along with Doris Day under her breath.

She didn't realize she'd pumped up the volume on her voice until she heard Debbie say, "Here is our kitchen songbird now."

Janet spotted Debbie at the entrance with two young women. One had gorgeous long black hair and an olive complexion. The other was a head taller and had a mop of wild shoulder-length curls. Janet scrambled for a joke to cover her embarrassment over being caught singing. "Hello." She set the plates on the counter. "I only entertain on Tuesdays, so lucky you for showing up when you did."

Debbie took the plates. "You'll be doing your tap routine next, right? I told Jasmine and Amber all about it. They'll be so disappointed if you don't dance for them."

The curly-haired woman bit her lip. Her companion cupped her hand over her mouth and looked away.

Debbie took the lunch specials to a couple by the window.

Janet dropped her hands to her sides. "Unfortunately, I forgot my tap shoes at home. You'll have to settle for my glorious voice." She made her way around the counter and over to the two young women. "You must be Debbie's renters. I'm Janet."

The shorter of the two held out her hand. "I'm Jasmine Greene."

Janet shook Jasmine's hand and turned to the other girl. "Let me guess. Amber."

"That's correct. Nice to meet you." Amber adjusted a bohemian style bag on her shoulder. "Debbie told us about her café, so we thought, why not have lunch here before unpacking?"

Jasmine started walking along the perimeter of the café, checking out the framed posters of Rosie the Riveter, the Christmas train, and World War II-era ads. "I'm glad we did. It's so cute. I love all the posters and the big band music."

Debbie came back over. "We're featuring big band music this month. If it turns out to be a hit, maybe we'll play it more often." She took two menus from the stack beside the cash register. She recommended a sunny table with a view of the train platform and one of the old engines.

Janet followed Debbie to the table. "I hear you'll be working with some of the residents at Good Shephard Retirement Center while you're here."

"We sure are." Amber accepted one of the menus from Debbie. "There are three teams involved in the project, thanks to a research grant. Each team will study two different communities—one small town and one big city. Then we'll compile our findings and present them at a symposium at the end August."

Jasmine took the other menu. "I practically begged to be Amber's partner when I found out she'd been assigned to Dennison and St. Louis. My great-grandfather grew up in Dennison. He passed away recently, so I thought it would be exciting to be where he once lived."

Janet tried to guess which family Jasmine might belong to. She appeared to be of part Indian descent, but if her last name was Greene, that ethnicity would probably be from her mother's side, and there had been a few generations between her great-grandfather and her. "What was your great-grandfather's name?"

"Bradley Macomb."

"Macomb doesn't sound familiar to me, but I bet you'll meet someone at Good Shepherd who knows the name."

Debbie set down fresh napkins. "Will you be working with all the residents at Good Shepherd or a select group?"

Jasmine rested her arms on top of her menu. Her eyes sparkled with intelligence. "Only a few that meet specific guidelines. We have a meeting set up with the center's director tomorrow morning to talk about residents who would be a good fit. We especially need subjects in their nineties or above who are physically healthy for their age and mentally sharp."

Debbie started adding utensils. "If you want some prime examples of longevity, be sure to include Ray Zink and Eileen Palmer. When you meet them, you'll think both are ten years younger than they really are. Ray is in a wheelchair, but don't let that fool you. He's one of the healthiest, sharpest people I know."

Janet prayed she wasn't overstepping with complete strangers. "If you're open to adding a participant outside Good Shepherd, I recommend talking to Harry Franklin as well. He just turned ninety-seven, still lives independently, and is a favorite of ours at the café."

"I think that would be fine to include him if he wants to participate. We only contacted Good Shepherd because we knew we'd find people in our target age bracket." Jasmine looked across the table at Amber, who gave a nod.

"Studying someone who still lives on his own at such an advanced age would be fascinating," said Amber.

What fascinated Janet was how quickly Jasmine and Amber had morphed from grad students on a road trip to professional researchers as soon as they started discussing their project. For a moment, Janet pictured Harry in a chair connected to probes monitoring his heart rate, blood oxygen level, and brain waves. Hearing words like *subjects* and *age bracket* reminded her why these bright young women had chosen to spend the first four weeks of a semester break in a small town: to study a cross section of Dennison's elderly population, not make Harry, Ray, and Eileen their new besties. Still, she knew Harry well enough to be assured that he would want to be included in anything that allowed him to get to know people, share his trade secrets to living well, and possibly educate nonlocals on the history of Dennison, the depot, and its deep connections to World War II.

Debbie's eyes moved to the window facing the depot. "Well, what do you know? I see Harry out in the depot right now, heading this way. He must have heard us talking about him. Before he comes in and I get distracted with introductions, can I get you girls something to drink? Iced tea? Lemonade? An Arnold Palmer so you can have a little of both?"

Jasmine's big brown eyes said, *Yum.* "An Arnold Palmer sounds good after our long drive."

"It does. I'll have the same."

"I'll be right back with those." Debbie patted Janet's arm. "I'll let you introduce Harry."

He came through the entrance with Crosby in tow.

Janet met them at the door. "Your timing is impeccable." She put her hand on his elbow. "I want you to meet Debbie's renters for this month." She led Harry to Jasmine and Amber's table. "This is Jasmine Greene and Amber Wells."

"Pleased to meet you both."

Crosby sat on his haunches, begging for attention.

Jasmine shifted around in her chair. "May I pet your dog?"

"He'd be disappointed if you didn't." Harry brought Crosby closer to the table.

"Hi, Crosby." Jasmine held out her hand to Crosby and let him sniff it. "What a great name."

Amber scooted her chair closer to Crosby and joined the admiration fest. "You are such a cutie."

Harry filled Jasmine and Amber in on Crosby's impressive heritage as a descendent of Bing the War Dog. "Bing's picture is the one featured in front of the museum ticket office."

Amber cupped Crosby's face. "No wonder you're so well behaved. You're a celebrity dog."

Debbie showed up with two tall glasses of iced tea mixed with lemonade. "Here you ladies go. Let me know when you need a refill." She smiled at Harry before glancing back to the students. "It's nice to see you so busy socializing that you haven't gotten to the menu yet."

Amber glanced in the direction of the specials board. Janet predicted that she would revert to the menu after seeing meat loaf as the lunch special. Amber didn't strike her as a meat loaf for lunch person. Neither did Jasmine. Sure enough, she flipped the menu open.

Jasmine kept her hand on Crosby's head and looked up at Harry. "What would you recommend, Harry? Janet said you're a regular here."

"Janet makes a mean BLT."

"I haven't had a BLT since high school." She handed her menu to Janet. "I'll have that. We're in a small-town café, so I'll let myself have some bacon."

"That's right," Harry said. "You can't have salad or a veggie burger in a place like this."

Debbie hovered a pen over her order pad. "Do you want fries or a side salad?"

Janet caught Harry mouthing *fries* to Jasmine.

Jasmine threw her hands up. "Why not go all out? I'll have the fries."

"That a girl." Harry gave Jasmine a big thumbs-up. "You can eat salads at home."

Amber moved her menu to the edge of the table. "What about a Cobb salad, Harry?"

Harry rubbed his index finger over his chin. "Let's see, bacon, blue cheese, hardboiled egg." He let his finger drop. "A Cobb salad passes."

"That's what I'll have then."

Debbie jotted down their order. "I'll take this to Paulette."

Crosby started inching his way closer to Jasmine. Harry drew him back a bit. "So, what brings you two to Dennison?"

"We're premed students." Jasmine unwrapped her straw. "Both hoping to specialize in geriatric care."

"You're in the right place. We have a nice-sized geriatric population in Dennison. At least according to our birth certificates."

Amber pulled her drink closer. "I hope we're not putting you on the spot, but Janet mentioned you might enjoy participating in our research project on longevity in the elderly."

"That sounds like an interesting project. If Janet here thinks it's a good think for Dennison, sign me up. Though I'm not sure I did anything special to earn as many years as I've been blessed with."

Janet considered how many steps Harry got in per day compared to the average person half his age. "Other than walking all over Dennison in any kind of weather and keeping his brain active with history trivia. Harry is not your typical ninety-seven-year-old."

Amber took a spiral notebook and ballpoint pen out of her tote bag. "We plan to do evaluations at Good Shepherd Retirement Center. If you fill out your name, phone number, and email address, we can send more information." She clipped the pen to the notebook cover and held it out to Harry.

"Sounds like a plan." Harry took the notebook.

Janet watched Crosby do his best to leave his new friends alone. "Harry, Jasmine's great-grandfather grew up in Dennison."

"Is that so? What's his name?"

Jasmine crumpled her straw wrapper. "Bradley Macomb. He moved decades ago and eventually ended up in Columbus, so I wouldn't be surprised if you don't remember him."

"I remember Bradley very well. Is he still with us?"

Sadness clouded Jasmine's expressive eyes. "He passed away last month. He was ninety-eight. One night he told Great-Grandma he didn't feel well and thought he'd go to bed early, and the next morning he was gone."

"Oh, I'm sorry to hear that. Bradley was a good man. I remember he fought in the Pacific."

"He was really special. I miss him a lot."

"If you ever want to hear some stories about Bradley, let me know. I'd be happy to share."

"I'd like that."

Harry excused himself to the next table over to write his contact information.

Janet gave Crosby a final pat on the head and left Jasmine and Amber to relax and enjoy their Arnold Palmers. She joined Paulette in the kitchen and found her crumbling bacon on Amber's Cobb salad.

"What can I do to help?"

Paulette pointed to the fryer with a half piece of bacon. "I haven't made the fries yet."

Janet went to the freezer for a bag of fries then scooped a generous serving into the basket. "I think Harry made a new friend. The great-grandfather of one of Debbie's renters used to live in Dennison. He's signing up for the longevity study right now."

"Harry is going to have a busy May between his float and being part of the longevity project."

Janet lowered the basket into the fryer. "Staying involved in the community is what keeps him young."

At three o'clock that afternoon, Janet rapped on the door of the house Debbie now shared with Greg, Jaxon, and Julian. She turned the knob, feeling the same freedom of open-door privileges as when Debbie lived in the craftsman-style home she bought from Ray Zink. "Hello, it's me."

"We're in the kitchen," Debbie called.

Janet shut the door just in time for Greg's border collie, Hammer, to come thundering down the stairs. "Hey, Hammer." Janet rubbed his lush black-and-white coat.

Between the entry hall and the kitchen, Janet noticed evidence of a woman's touch in a house dominated by males. Flowers on one end table in the living room, the fragrance of lavender, even a smattering of throw pillows on the sofa. She found Debbie and Paulette in various stages of coffee preparation and a mug waiting for her on the counter beside a new coffee maker. Her cookbook sat beside the stove, propped on a stand.

Janet stopped to enjoy seeing her gift on display.

"I just showed your book off to Paulette," Debbie said.

Paulette tapped a teaspoon on the side of her mug. "And Paulette is extremely impressed."

"Thank you. The hardest part was keeping it secret." Janet examined the high-end coffee gadget. "Fancy." The machine had a tray for resting a mug in addition to a place for a carafe. It could make one cup at a time or a whole pot. "I want one of these." Not that it was in her budget.

"I have Paulette to thank for my newfangled machine." Debbie handed Janet the empty mug. "Try it out. It's fun." She opened a drawer under the coffee maker, filled with a selection of pods. "Tada!"

"It also steams milk." Paulette stirred sugar into her coffee. She gave the coffee maker a pat. "This was a late wedding gift. I could not have my new daughter-in-law drinking out of Greg's man-cave carafe."

Debbie smiled at her. "My dream has come true. I have a mother-in-law who likes me."

"You have a mother-in-law who adores you."

Janet chose a pod of Hawaiian Blend because it sounded like a vacation in a cup. Debbie and Paulette puttered around the kitchen looking like they'd been family forever.

Debbie poured a generous helping of half-and-half into her mug. "How about if we brainstorm in the living room?"

Janet watched the last spurt of coffee drip into her mug. "Sounds good." She added half-and-half and sugar then followed Debbie and Paulette.

"We'll have the house to ourselves." Debbie led the way into the living room. "The boys are meeting Greg after school to figure out how to make their idea for the Connor Construction float a reality."

Janet settled herself into the corner seat of Debbie's sofa. She found a coaster and set it on the end table. "I have an idea for our float." She'd tried coming up with other options since Greg's announcement but always came back to the same one. "What if we recreate the old Salvation Army Canteen?"

"I love it! Greg has a flatbed we could use. The main thing we would need is a rectangular table, serving trays, and some old coffee pitchers."

Paulette took a sip. "I have a wooden table in the garage that would fit on a flatbed. It's a little beat up, but with a coat of paint and tightening one wobbly leg, it'll be just what we need."

Debbie moved her drink to the coffee table. "It'll need to be bolted to the flatbed."

Paulette waved a hand at Debbie. "Do anything you want to it. Right now its only purpose is holding items I should've donated ages ago."

"Perfect. Thank you so much, Paulette." Janet formed a picture in her mind of what the Salvation Army Canteen tables usually included. "We need a row of sack lunches. We wouldn't need to put real food in them, just something to make them look full."

Debbie took a pad of paper and a pen from the coffee table. "I'll start the list of supplies. So far, we need lunch sacks, paint, coffee-pots, and serving trays. And of course some decorations."

"I'll volunteer to look for serving trays and coffeepots." Paulette moved a throw pillow to her lap. "Should we pass out doughnuts to the crowd? I feel like we need to pass something out if we're going to make the canteen authentic."

Janet took another sip of coffee and considered how they could make that work. Someone would need to be at the table to make the canteen realistic. "We could do it if one of us walks along each side of the float to hand them out while the other stays by the table. We can put the doughnuts in little bags and toss them into the crowd." She imagined baggies flying through the air, ready to be caught. Then she pictured one landing with a splat and an eager child opening her bag to find a broken doughnut. "Or maybe handing them out is better."

Debbie wrote quickly.

Janet recalled the recipe for the Salvation Army doughnuts. It was extremely simple thanks to wartime resourcefulness. "I'll get started making them this weekend and freeze them."

Debbie tapped her pen on the pad. She shook her head. "Wait. Let's think about how many doughnuts you'd have to make. It wouldn't be like baking a day's worth for the café."

Paulette started counting silently on her fingers. "Ingredients will add up too. Let's scratch the doughnuts."

"But the Salvation Army doughnuts were famous. We have to include some." Janet did a quick calculation in her head. Events with historical significance drew the whole community plus people from surrounding towns. She imagined herself sweating over a pot of hot oil with a growing pile of doughnuts behind her, on each side of the stove, in corners of the café kitchen. *I wouldn't be making them for everyone at the parade.* "I can manage, say, a hundred—enough to pass out along the parade route. I'll make mini ones to stretch each batch."

"If Janet's willing, let's go for it." Debbie wrote, underlined, and ended with a sharp dot of her pen.

Paulette kicked off her shoes and swung her stockinged feet up onto the couch. "What about costumes? I bet we all have something from past events to re-wear."

Debbie tapped her notepad with the pen. "Volunteers would've worn the same dresses over and over again anyway. We could freshen up past costumes with new scarves and accessories."

Janet knew exactly where to get what Debbie had in mind. "I'll drop into Jenny's Thrifts this week." She could do it before her coffee date with Mandy.

Paulette slapped her knees. "Next time we meet, we can plan decorations. For now, we can pray that everyone's float comes together without a hitch."

CHAPTER FOUR

Harry arrived at the depot for his Monday afternoon shift with almost ten minutes to spare. It felt strange to know that in only a few weeks he would be free to work during school hours.

After storing his dinner pail in his locker and buttoning his porter's coat, he took advantage of the final few minutes to talk to Miss Eileen. He found her in the stationmaster's office, writing in her logbook. A small, framed picture of her with Rafe Palmer sat in the back corner of her desk.

Harry knocked on the doorframe, his porter hat still in his hand.

Miss Eileen turned in her swivel chair. "Hi, Harry. What can I do for you?"

"If you have a minute, I'd like to run an idea by you. It has to do with the float you asked me and Sylvia to help you with."

"I'm happy to hear any ideas you have."

"On Saturday, Sylvia and I saw Mitch's brother, Bradley, in town and thought it might be nice to invite him to help. He won a sculpting award in high school, so Sylvia thought we could use his artistic mind."

Miss Eileen sat silent for a moment. Harry predicted she might be thinking the same thing he did when Sylvia suggested recruiting Bradley.

"I know Bradley doesn't work for the depot, but he used to."

Harry waited for Miss Eileen to bring up Bradley's blindness.

"I think that's a wonderful idea, Harry. As Dad has said so often, a person needs a sense of purpose."

"I'll ask him during my break."

Miss Eileen turned back to her desk then toward Harry again. "It was thoughtful of Sylvia to think of Bradley. It pleases me to see you and Sylvia together. You seem like a good match."

Harry had no doubt about that. Being with Sylvia felt natural and easy. He could talk to her about anything, and something about her spunky spirit made him want to be braver. "I think—I know—I've found *the girl I want to marry." He looked over his shoulder, at the off chance that Sylvia decided to drop by the station. The coast was clear. "I've already started saving for an engagement ring. But before I even think about buying it or bringing up marriage, I want to know I can provide for a family."*

Harry had had many talks with his father about what it took to support a wife, keep the rent paid, lights on and food on the table, and raise children. He'd seen families in his neighborhood struggle, and his own family had seen their share of hard times, but his father had always set a good example of how to provide by working hard and being careful with money. He knew his job at the depot was his ticket to steady work, and Harry's goal of becoming a conductor had never faded. "Now that I have three years as a porter under my belt, I'm hoping to start working my way up."

"I feel confident you'll meet that goal, Harry. For the first step, you ought to apply for a porter position on one of the routes. It'll mean being on the train for a week at a time, but it's a step toward what you want to do."

"Thank you, Miss Eileen."

"I'll let you know when I hear of an opening. And I'd be happy to put in a letter of recommendation for you when one comes up."

Harry gripped his hat with both hands. "I'd sure appreciate that. For now, I better clock in for the job I already have."

The afternoon seemed slower than in the past when troop trains kept the depot hopping. But Harry still managed to keep himself busy until early evening. A westbound train was due for a stop in Dennison at half past five. He pulled a luggage cart to the doors leading to the platform to prepare for the train's arrival. Through the window, he spotted a white cane sticking out from the bench closest to the entrance. He opened the door and kicked down the doorstop. While pulling out the cart, he saw Bradley sitting alone on the bench.

If he didn't know for certain that Bradley lost his sight in Japan, he would think the young man was watching the tracks for the next incoming train. He'd been sitting on the bench a half hour ago too when Harry went outside to sweep the platform.

"Hi, Bradley. Can I help you with something?"

"No thanks." Bradley's gaze stayed fixed. "Just getting some fresh air."

Judging from the sound of his voice, Bradley needed some encouragement as much as fresh air.

Footsteps behind him drew Harry away from concern for Bradley.

Miss Eileen took hold of the other end of the cart while Harry rolled it out onto the platform. "I just got word that the westbound train is running thirty minutes behind schedule. How about if you take your dinner break now, so you'll be around when it arrives?"

"Sure. I'd be happy to."

Miss Eileen said hello to Bradley. She snapped her stationmaster watch closed and slipped it into her front pocket. Harry followed her inside. His hand lingered on the door handle.

"Is something wrong, Harry? You look distracted."

"Nothing's wrong. It's just that Bradley has been sitting out there for a while. I imagine it's hard having so much time on his hands." Especially while his younger brother worked at the depot.

Miss Eileen took a quick glance out the window. "It's sad to see so many of our veterans struggling to find work because of injuries. I watched my own father struggle after being injured in the Great War. They served their country, and now they can't provide for their families, or even for themselves."

"I'm happy that we can give him something to do, even if it's only volunteering to help with a float."

"We never know what a little opportunity will do for a person's morale."

Harry went to the back room for his dinner pail and stopped at the water cooler to fill a cup. He thought of Bradley and filled a second cup for him. At the door, he balanced both cups in one hand then stepped outside. He could feel the fresh evening breeze. Nights were getting a little later as spring made way for summer with its evenings balmy enough to stroll past dark, watch the stars, and make Saturday night ice cream.

Harry found Bradley where he last saw him, on the bench closest to the entrance. He noticed a sadness on his face.

"Hello again, Bradley. It's Harry. Can I join you?"

"Sure." Bradley moved his cane aside to make room for Harry.

"I brought you a cup of water."

"That's kind of you. Thanks." Bradley held out his hand, and Harry put the cup into it.

Harry took a seat on the opposite side of the bench. He set his cup on the ground. "The next train's running late." Harry opened his dinner pail and took out the sandwich he'd made using leftover meat loaf from Sunday supper and his mother's homemade white bread. He could smell the spices his mom used. They made ordinary meat loaf taste like a fancy meal for company. The aroma made his stomach growl. But the thought of eating in front of Bradley didn't sit right.

Harry unwrapped the wax paper around his sandwich and held it out to Bradley. "Would you like half?"

Bradley shook his head. "I don't want to take your food."

"Go ahead. I was a little greedy with the leftover meat loaf. Half will be plenty for me." He picked up one half and held it out to Bradley. He felt his face flush over the embarrassing realization that he'd held the half out as if Bradley could see it.

"Well, it does smell good. Maybe I will."

Harry set the wrapped half on the bench seat. "It's right beside you on the left."

"Thanks."

They sat in silence for a moment, chewing and listening to the sounds of evening. Until Bradley said, "Sylvia seems like a sweet girl."

"She's the best. Of course, I'm sure Margo is the best in your opinion."

Bradley's lips spread into a smile. "Everyone thinks his girl is the best."

Harry bit into his sandwich while trying to figure out how to introduce the idea of Bradley helping with the float. He couldn't very well say, "Sylvia and I were talking about you and..." Sylvia's story about seeing Bradley's picture in the art room at school came back to him. "Sylvia says you won a pretty impressive award *for sculpting in high school. She saw your picture in the art room at our school."*

Bradley swallowed and nodded. *"I won for a wooden carving of our Irish setter, Sean, running for a stick."* He lowered his eyes and wiped breadcrumbs off his lips. *"That was a long time ago."*

"It's still something to be proud of. I'm not very artistic. I admire people who are."

Bradley took a sip of his water. *"It's interesting how things turn out. Before I joined the army, I wanted to go to art school after graduation. I had this big dream of becoming a famous sculptor like Michelangelo. But my dad kept pushing me to pursue medicine instead. He thought I would make a good surgeon. When I told him I wanted to study sculpting, he said he couldn't justify wasting money on a 'namby-pamby art school,' as he put it. We got in a big argument over it."* He set his cup on the bench, but his fingers didn't move from it. *"Now I can't do either."*

Harry looked down at his half-eaten sandwich. *"I'm sure sorry, Bradley."* Maybe that was one blessing to Harry's decision to not pursue college but to aim for a conductor's position. He and his parents didn't have career choices to argue about. As far back as Harry could remember, his mom and dad had supported every effort he made to earn his own money, whether it was doing odd jobs or working at the depot. He wished he could assure Bradley that he would find a new path eventually.

"It's not your fault." Bradley lifted his sandwich to his lips. "It's the war's fault."

"I know. But I'm sorry you got injured. I'm sorry that the war changed your life like this."

It had changed Ray Zink's too. Not as profoundly as Bradley's, but he'd been injured. His girl hadn't kept her promise to wait.

"Me too." Bradley's voice sounded tight. Once again, Harry noticed a far-off expression on Bradley's face.

"You know, Miss Eileen asked me and Sylvia to help create a depot float for the Honor Parade and Picnic that's happening at the end of the month. We need all the help we can get. We'd like to have you on our committee if you have time."

"I don't know, Harry."

"You're an award-winning artist, after all."

Bradley smirked. "I can't see enough to sculpt or build anything."

Harry borrowed Sylvia's comment from Saturday. "But your artistic mind still works just fine, I'm sure."

"You mean it?"

"I wouldn't ask if we didn't. It was Sylvia who thought of it."

Bradley ran his thumb over the wax paper around his sandwich. "It would be nice to be involved in something. I'm not sure how much I'll be able to contribute. I haven't tried anything creative since coming home."

Harry didn't want to set Bradley up for a situation where he felt in the way, or like they asked him out of pity. Then something came to him. "It would be great if you could help us come up with a theme. I have no idea where to start when it comes to designing a float. If you managed to turn a block of wood into a dog that was realistic enough to win first place, I bet you could come up with an idea for a float."

Bradley stared off into the distance. Something in his face changed, like the invitation to be part of a project had awakened the artist in him. "A float for a train opens all kinds of possibilities. You could create an engine, a passenger car." He shifted his body around. "Or, for an honor parade, how about a troop car? I left Dennison on one and returned on another. Every soldier in Dennison can say the same."

Harry set the rest of his sandwich aside. "Bradley, that's it. Instead of going off to fight, the boys are finally coming home for good."

CHAPTER FIVE

On Thursday afternoon, Janet draped her tote bag across her shoulder and turned the kitchen over to Paulette. "I'm off to the thrift store to look for scarves and things. Then I'm having a coffee date with my friend Mandy. I'll send pictures from the store if I find anything else promising."

Paulette flipped a patty melt on the griddle. "I wish I'd kept some of my mother's dresses after she passed. I never thought about storing them away to use as costumes."

"My mom said the same thing when we were talking about the parade." Janet hung her gingham apron on a hook. "Then we started reminiscing about Grandma's signature dresses, realized how often we saw her in the same ones, and decided it was just as well that Mom let someone from her publishing company cut the usable fabric into squares for quilting."

The oven timer went off.

"I'm sure the same is true of Mother's wardrobe. She wore everything to death." Paulette waved an oven-mitted hand. "Have fun with your friend."

"I will. Mandy is always up to something exciting. She managed a bistro with her late husband for a while, got her master's while raising twins. No doubt, we'll have a lot to talk about."

After a successful trip to the thrift store that provided three scarves, three pairs of chunky clip-on earrings, artificial flower pins for whatever needed some pizzazz, and a pillbox hat that would look great on Paulette, Janet pulled into a parking space in front of Totally Awesome Coffee. Before she opened the door, she found the place overrun with high school kids. As expected, the inside screamed 1985, with its black-and-white-checked floor, framed posters of one-hit wonders, and a popular tune from Janet's childhood playing over the sound system. She looked around for Mandy.

Mandy's voice called to Janet from behind. "Janet, over here."

Janet turned around and found her at a small round table in a corner near the bar where customers could find napkins, cup sleeves, and cinnamon shakers. "*Phew.* When I saw the crowd, I was worried we wouldn't be able to get a table."

Mandy got up from her chair and held her arms out to Janet. "It's so good to see you."

"It's good to see you too." Janet embraced Mandy. She'd updated her style with a short sassy haircut. "You look incredible. Thanks so much for reaching out."

"When I found out I was going to be in the area, you were the first person who came to mind." Mandy pulled a cute herringbone tweed wallet out of her purse. "Should I order for us while you save the table? I'm buying."

"Thanks." Janet looked up at the menu full of names that reminded her of cutting necks and sleeves off sweatshirts to create a costume almost every year for '80s Days at Tiffany's schools. She spotted a blended iced mocha called Big Hair that boasted extra high whipped cream and decided the name was too funny to pass up. She had a flashback to watching the cafeteria lady at school pass out hot lunches and wondering how she got her bangs so high.

Mandy settled on a berry smoothie called Neon Pink. "I have a feeling it'll taste like fruity sugar cereal, but who cares? I feel like I'm in elementary school again."

By the time Mandy ordered and came back to the table with their drinks, Janet had taken a picture of the menu and texted it to Debbie. THIS PLACE IS PACKED! THE AVERAGE CUSTOMER WAS BORN LONG AFTER THE 80S ENDED.

Debbie replied, A GOOD SIGN THEY MAKE GREAT COFFEE.

Mandy set Janet's drink in front of her. "The 'big' in the name of your iced mocha was not an exaggeration."

Janet shifted back at the sight of a six-inch spray of whipped cream dotted with chocolate sprinkles. "Oh my word. I could cover half a cream pie with that."

Mandy returned to her chair and popped a straw into her smoothie. "I'm not sure I want to know what made the pink in my drink possible." She took a sip. "But it sure is yummy." She took a quick trip to the napkin dispenser and wiped pink off her lips. "What have you been up to?"

Janet tried her mocha—a bit on the sweet side but otherwise delicious. She reached for one of the napkins. "I'm keeping busy running the café with Debbie Albright. Excuse me, Debbie Connor. She just got married. We opened almost two years ago and already have a steady flow of regulars."

Mandy rolled her straw wrapper into a perfect little tube and set it aside. "I looked the Whistle Stop Café up online after we talked on Monday night. It's darling. I'll make a point to stop in while I'm here."

"So, you mentioned teaching a class."

"I'm helping with a pastry intensive in Barnhill."

"I didn't know Barnhill had a culinary school. It must be brand-new."

"It's an extension of the baker's academy in Vermillion and uses focused intensives rather than full semesters. It opened in February. I found out about it through a friend. Now that Leslie and Leanna are away at college and I feel more settled, it's a good challenge."

Janet fought for words. In the three years since Gary passed, she'd only been able to express her sympathy in cards and brief messages. Mandy appeared to be in a place where she wanted to dwell on her life now instead of Gary's death, but it didn't feel right to avoid acknowledging such a loss. "Mandy, I'm so glad you have an exciting opportunity after what happened with Gary. I think he would be happy for you."

"I'm positive he would be."

"How long is the pastry intensive?"

"Through the end of May." Mandy leaned forward. "Guess where I'm teaching next?"

"Le Cordon Bleu?"

Mandy laughed. "Not quite. I got invited to teach at the London School of Cookery."

"That sounds very posh."

"They have a pretty prestigious baking program. I'm teaching for fall semester as a guest instructor."

"How did that come about?" Mandy had always been one of those never-met-a-stranger types. It didn't shock Janet a bit to know Mandy had found connections that led her abroad.

"Through the same friend who told me about the baking academy. Her name is Glenis. We met while taking a vegetarian cooking class of all things, at a gourmet kitchen store that offered courses. A friend gave it to me for my birthday after Gary died. Glenis was a professional baker originally from England, and we hit it off immediately. She's also a widow, so when she found out I had recently become one, she took me under her wing. When she returned to the UK, she invited me to spend a couple of weeks with her. That's when she told me she'd gotten a job overseeing the baking program at the School of Cookery and invited me to apply for a special course."

"I'm ecstatic for you. England. How many people get to put that on their résumé?"

"I fell in love with England when I visited Glenis. Have you ever been there?"

Janet shook her head and sipped her coffee drink. Whipped cream collided with her nose. She wiped it off. "Ian and I have stayed pretty close to home. I guess you can say we support Ohio's economy." She'd even gone to college close to home. An hour and forty minutes away, to be exact. She'd driven back every weekend the first year because she missed her family and her own bed. Meeting Mandy during sophomore year gave her a reason to stay on campus more. Then Mandy did a semester abroad, and she started going home weekly again until her friend got back.

"I highly recommend getting out in the world, at least a bit. When I visited Glenis, I came home with all kinds of baking inspiration.

New recipes, ideas for jazzing up boring ones. In February, I went to France for a chocolate making class. It was life changing."

The idea of baking inspiration sank into Janet's mind. She'd never considered the advantages of seeing other parts of the world for the purpose of expanding her skills and repertoire. "Does this cookery school offer online courses? Maybe I'll sign up for one."

"No, unfortunately. They believe a hands-on in-person experience is best for cooking and baking."

Janet snapped her fingers. "Oh well." It would be challenging to fit in an intensive course around café hours anyway.

"Too bad the program I'm teaching for is full. I would encourage you to register. You could start offering Victoria sponge cake at the café, and say you learned your secrets for getting it right in London."

Janet imagined what a Victoria sponge would look like in the café's bakery case. Very nice with its signature heavy cream and jam sandwiched between two round yellow cakes and topped with powdered sugar.

Mandy stirred her neon drink. "Glenis started a wait list. Do you want me to ask her to add your name?"

The idea of attending school in London sounded like something out of a movie. So exciting. And completely impossible. "I couldn't leave the café for that long." She pictured her regular customers sticking their forks through the delicate layers of Victoria sponge. As lovely as the cake would look in the case, it didn't quite match her customer base. "Our locals are more into comfort food than fancy cakes anyway."

"How do you know if you don't offer them something different?"

"For this month, all our special offerings are from 1945 to celebrate the end of World War II. But maybe I'll try something more upscale on them in June."

Janet told Mandy about the big Memorial Day celebration. She described the float she, Debbie, and Paulette were planning for. Suddenly, a recreated canteen and running up the parade route passing out mini doughnuts sounded downhome and dated compared to a semester in London.

Janet was still mulling over Mandy's teaching news and how much she wished she could add her name to the waiting list at the London School of Cookery when she heard the garage door open. She hunched over a recipe for chicken with dates and olives. All the talk about fine baking had sent her home determined to make something for dinner that sounded exotic.

She reminded herself of the deep loss that came before Mandy's chance to teach overseas. *I'd rather have Ian alive and well than go anywhere in the world.*

Ian dropped his key fob into the dish beside his phone charger. "Good evening, my love."

Janet set her cookbook on the counter. "Hello, darling."

Ian plugged the charging cable into his phone. "So, I'm curious. What exactly is wrong with people?"

"Do you mean society in general, or someone who cut you off on the way home?" She got up to search the pantry for dates, as if those had ever found their way onto her weekly shopping list. "In which case, it takes a lot of nerve to cut off a police officer in a town where you're likely to run into him in the grocery store the next day."

Ian leaned against the pantry doorframe. "The headlights for our Military Police Cruiser float disappeared sometime between last night and this afternoon."

Janet found a bag of raisins and a packet of dried cranberries. "Oh no." She grabbed both.

Ian followed Janet to the counter. "Whoever took the lights replaced them with those novelty bulbs that look like they're melting."

Janet pressed her lips together to keep from cracking up over the mental image of melting light bulbs. She snorted before she could stop herself. "Sorry. I shouldn't mock your pain. But that's hilarious. Did the bulbs have faces on them?"

"No, they did not have faces on them." Janet heard a burst of repressed amusement escape through Ian's lips. "Great, now that image is in my head. Thanks a lot." Ian took his wallet out of his front pocket and tossed it on the counter. "It wasn't irreparable damage, just a nuisance that required a trip to the supply room for another set of headlights. What bugs me is that it happened right under our noses, in the back parking lot of the police station."

Janet ran her index finger down the list of ingredients for the chicken dish. *Kalamata olives.* Green olives would have to do. "I wonder if it's a senior prank. They were warned to stop, but there's always that outlier."

"Could be." Ian got a glass out of the cabinet.

Janet went to the refrigerator for an extra jar of green olives she'd bought for an Easter charcuterie board. She could switch out the dates with raisins. One more light bulb jab made its way into her head. "I bet you'll find the headlights someplace unexpected tomorrow. That's when the crazy faces will come in. Check the toilet paper dispensers in the men's room."

Janet pictured a giant toilet paper holder with a grinning, googly-eyed light bulb screwed into the side of it and erupted into a belly laugh.

Ian finished filling his glass with water. He shut off the tap with a firm twist. "Are you the culprit? You seem to know an awful lot about what I can expect next."

"No." Janet yanked open the zipper seal on the raisin bag. "I have a solid alibi in case you're about to launch an investigation into my activities. Today, I went from the café to Jenny's Thrifts, to Totally Awesome Coffee to meet Mandy, where she made me desperately jealous over an upcoming teaching gig in London." She thrust her thumb over her shoulder. "The evidence is in the shopping bag beside my purse. You'll find an array of out-of-style accessories and a brochure from the coffee place." She plunked the jar of olives on her favorite wooden cutting board.

"No need. I believe you."

"Maybe it's someone in the force trying to be funny."

Ian opened the jar and returned it to the board. He took a fork from the utensils drawer and used it to skewer two olives. "If that's the case, when I find out who did it, my revenge will be sweet."

CHAPTER SIX

Dennison, Ohio
May 10, 1946

Harry watched Sylvia walk the perimeter of the old Ford truck that a friend of Mr. Rafe's had offered for the depot float. She strolled over to an out-of-use passenger car and ran her hand along the side. "It's too bad this is too big to pull behind the truck."

Bradley extended his cane and joined Sylvia beside the passenger car. Harry glanced over at Miss Eileen then back at Bradley. He held himself back from blurting out, "How did you know where Sylvia was?" In the few days he'd spent with Bradley, he'd caught on that the young man had been trained well to listen and take advantage of the small amount of sight he had.

Bradley touched the dark gray panels and reached up to one of the windows. "How about using the bed of the truck as the passenger car? We could build a frame out of wood to fit around the bed and over the cab and paint it to match. What color is the Ford?"

"Blue," Eileen said. "But Rafe's friend said we're free to paint it if need be. He only uses it for hauling."

"So he won't mind if we paint it fire-engine red?" Bradley turned around. Based on his cheeky grin, Harry sensed he'd gotten his sense of humor back since looking so forlorn on the bench outside the depot.

"Um."

"I'm just joking, Miss Eileen. We can leave it as is, paint the wood gray, and build it in a way that covers the sides of the truck."

Harry tried to picture what Bradley described. "Would we cut out windows or paint them on?"

Bradley put one hand on his waist. He stared down at the ground. "Cutouts would be more realistic."

Sylvia folded her arms across her chest. "That could work." Her dark eyes fixed on the old truck then on the old passenger car.

Miss Eileen wandered over to stand next to her. "What's on your mind, Sylvia? I see the wheels in your brain turning."

Sylvia dropped her arms to her sides, still staring at the passenger car. She shifted her eyes to the truck.

"I like this idea of creating a troop car, but how will we make it obvious that the soldiers are coming home?"

Harry tried to recall the parade his family had gone to in Akron right after VJ Day. Many of the groups carried celebratory signs or banners. "We could make a Welcome Home banner."

Sylvia leaned against the old passenger car. "I like that. But I think we should do even more. For a celebration of such a long war coming to an end, the float needs to be extra special."

Bradley got a keen look that Harry remembered seeing on Bradley sometimes before the war. "We need a focal point, you mean?"

"That's the word." Sylvia went over to the blue Ford and around to the front of it. "The trouble is nothing specific comes to mind."

Bradley made his way over to the truck. He stopped at the lefthand side of the bed and rested both palms on the edge. "When I was in the hospital and told other men I was from Dennison, some told me they'd traveled through this station on their way to being shipped overseas. They all talked about being treated warmly during the most uncertain time in their life. Welcomed with homemade cookies and sandwiches and kind smiles." He turned around and rested his *back against the truck bed. "Their stories made me so homesick. They reminded me I'd come from some-where that made a difference to people. This place was a light. Maybe we could add a focal point that reflects that theme. A welcoming light."*

Harry pictured a candle or a lamp, neither of which would show up when they needed it to. "The parade will be during the day."

"You're right." Bradley tapped the side of the truck. "Let me think on it."

Bradley seemed like a different man than the one who responded to Harry's invitation to help by remind-ing him, "I can't see." Harry sensed that he'd found what Eileen's father talked about—a sense of purpose.

Miss Eileen checked her pocket watch. "I better get back inside. The five-thirty train is arriving in ten minutes." She looked around the area leading to the depot. "I don't see Mitch anywhere. He was due to clock in at five. He's never late."

Bradley pulled away from the truck. "This morn-ing at breakfast, he mentioned meeting with one of his teachers after school to ask for help. Maybe it took lon-ger than expected. Though it's not like him to shrug off being on time for work."

Harry looked toward the depot. "Maybe he went inside while we were talking, and we didn't see him."

"I'll probably run into him the minute I go inside." Miss Eileen started walking to the depot.

She had barely made it to the platform when Harry saw Mitch coming down the street, walking his bike instead of riding it. The pattern of his steps indicated he might have fallen off and gotten injured. Harry ran over to meet him.

"Mitch, are you okay?"

Mitch rolled his bike up the gravel walkway leading to the depot. "I hit a pothole. It's my own fault. I was in a rush to get here after going home to drop off my books and change into my uniform."

Harry heard Sylvia's voice behind him, guiding Bradley around a lamp post.

Bradley caught up to his brother. "Are you hurt?"

"Just banged up a little. Nothing to worry about." Mitch held out his left arm. "Except it looks like I tore my jacket."

Sylvia checked the arm of Mitch's porter coat. "You sure did."

"Mitch, what happened to you?" Miss Eileen shouted from the platform.

Bradley filled her in.

"Come on inside. I'll find the first aid kit."

Harry examined Mitch's torn jacket and rattled expression. "Go on. I'll cover for you this evening."

"I'll be fine as soon as I get cleaned up." Mitch tipped his bike to one side. "I don't know about my bike though. When I fell, I broke the chain, and knocked the bottom bracket and pedal all out of whack."

Bradley took hold of one of the handlebars. "Let me take a look at it." He reached out to touch his brother's arm. "Go get yourself cleaned up. I'll take care of your bike."

Mitch rubbed his arm. "If you can't fix it, I know what I'll be spending my next paycheck on. The bike repair shop."

"Nah." Bradley waved him off. "I'll get it taken care of."

Miss Eileen met Mitch halfway down the path. "I'll loan you a spare jacket until we can get yours mended."

"Thanks, Miss Eileen."

Bradley waited until Mitch reached the platform to ask Harry, "Can you show me where to find some tools?"

Sylvia spoke up. "Come with me. I'll take you to the repair shed. I used to work here as a mechanic." She held out her elbow for Bradley to take and offered to hold his cane while he pushed Mitch's bike. She shouted to Harry, "I'll check the lumberyard near my house for some siding boards we can use."

Harry watched Sylvia usher Bradley out toward the repair shed. He said a prayer that Bradley would be able to do the repairs so Mitch wouldn't have to spend a paycheck sending it to the shop. Another prayer flowed out for Bradley. *God, it seems important to him to get the repair job done himself. Please help him out.*

Once Mitch had patched himself up, Harry clocked out and changed into regular clothes so he and Sylvia could get started on finding boards before it was time to go home for supper. He left his uniform in his locker for his next shift. On his way to leave for the lumber-yard, he wandered over to the repair shed designated for smaller jobs. He found Bradley sitting on the floor of the shed with Mitch's bike propped up against the righthand side wall and a box of tools to his left.

"How's it coming along?"

"So far so good."

On the worktable behind Bradley, Harry saw an old lantern. He recognized it from when Miss Eileen had asked him to take it to the repair shed. The latch for the section that usually swung open when changing the light had broken during the holidays. Now the latch appeared fine. Harry went over for a look. Not only had someone fixed the latch, but they'd tightened the hinge and dusted the entire lantern. "This lamp is as good as new."

Bradley reached into the toolbox, felt around, and pulled out a wrench. "I hope no one minds that I tinkered with it a bit. Sylvia told me where to find the tools and rags for the bike, and I found that lamp beside the toolbox. It made me think about our need for a focal point for our float. The next thing I knew I was polishing it up. My mind has always wanted to sort out ideas by working with my hands."

Harry picked up the lantern to examine the details. "I doubt anyone will mind." He would never have known that the person who polished and repaired it could barely see.

Bradley removed the pedal from the bent bottom bracket of Mitch's bike. "Too bad I don't have metal-working tools. I could work some magic on that lantern. Maybe etch a design that creates a nice effect when the light shines through it." He got to his feet and put his hand out until he found the long wooden work surface against the back wall. "That bracket is bent pretty badly." He gently tapped the pedal on the table. Then he set it down. "Do you know where I can find a piece of pipe about this big around?" He made a circle with his thumb and index finger. "And something to wrap around the bracket? Even a large rag will do if it's clean."

Harry looked around until he found some wrapping for protecting pipes in winter. He spotted a piece of piping in a box of scrap metal.

As he looked, he noticed another lantern on a table in the corner of the work shed. It was one of the large types that stationmasters used for alerting train conductors in bad weather. He had no idea how long it had sat on that table collecting cobwebs and dust, its broken parts unattended and forgotten. He imagined what it might look like if someone spruced it up and added the etchings that Bradley thought would be nice on the smaller lantern he'd polished.

Harry gave Bradley the pipe and wrapping. He observed as Bradley wound the wrapping around the bracket, yanked it tight, slipped the pipe over the rag, gripped the pipe with one hand while holding the bracket with the other, and slowly but firmly tugged the bracket straight. He sat back on his knees and ran his hand over the surface of the bracket. "That'll do for now. I can still feel a dent, but I can smooth that out at home."

Harry's eyes returned to the old stationmaster's lantern.

Harry found Sylvia in the lumberyard comparing one piece of siding against another. With the images of the old lantern and Bradley repairing Mitch's bike still fresh in his mind, he felt like he couldn't get the story out fast enough.

With each detail he recounted, Sylvia's face became brighter. She abandoned the boards and grabbed Harry's arm. "Let's go tell Miss Eileen before she leaves for the night."

By the time they reached the depot again, Harry could feel his shirt sticking to his back, but he didn't care. Sylvia stopped outside Miss Eileen's office and caught her breath.

"Everything okay out there?" Miss Eileen came to the door. "I thought you two left already."

Harry wiped his brow with the back of his hand. "Miss Eileen, do you have a minute?"

"I have a few minutes. What can I do for you?"

Harry motioned for Sylvia to follow him into the office.

"Sylvia and I have an idea for how to add a focal point to the float and give Bradley something meaningful to do."

Eileen sat in her desk chair. "Wonderful. What's the idea?"

Harry told Eileen what he'd seen Bradley do in the repair shed, and about the old lantern.

"If Bradley can spruce up the stationmaster lantern and add a nice design, it could give our float the special touch it needs," Miss Eileen said.

She swived her chair back and forth with her feet. "If it's where I think it is, that lantern was probably destined for scrap metal."

Harry felt like a little kid again, begging his dad if he could turn an old tire into a swing. "So it's okay if we use it?"

"I don't see why not if it's no longer in use."

Sylvia's excitement took over the office. "It would be front and center. I'm picturing you walking in front of the float, holding the lantern. Way up high." Her hands flew like a fine actress delivering a monologue. "I'm picturing ribbons and flowers on it. Like you're guiding the troops home. Harry and I will be behind you with a welcome home banner for the veterans."

Miss Eileen sat quietly for a moment. "Do you think Bradley is up to the job? What you said he would like to do with the other lantern sounds like a piece of art. But wishing and doing are two different things."

Harry recapped watching Bradley fix the bike bracket without asking for any assistance except to hand over a piece of pipe. How confident he sounded when he wished he had access to tools for etching a design into a lantern that no one cared to fix until he did. "I'm sure he would be up for it."

"Okay then. He's hired."

CHAPTER SEVEN

On Friday evening, Janet nestled on the couch with her big gray kitty, Ranger, while Laddie snored in his dog bed across the room. Despite a shower and thorough washing, her hands still bore a few specks of the cream-colored paint she and Debbie had used to freshen up Paulette's old table for the parade float.

Ian came in with two mugs of decaf tea. "I just got a text from Tiffany." He set one mug on the end table beside Janet. "She's on schedule to arrive on Sunday around noon. She's bringing pizza and a salad for lunch, so you don't have to cook on Mother's Day."

"I love that girl." Janet moved her feet off the couch to make room for Ian, careful not to disturb Ranger's snooze. She wrapped her fingers around her mug and blew into the hot tea. "I'm sure she'll also have a big pile of laundry."

Ian laid a coaster on the coffee table for his mug. "You might see a little less of me over the next few weeks. The force drafted me to lead the float committee. They're hoping my presence will prevent future problems with the float."

Janet stroked Ranger's back. "Have you confirmed if the head-light incident was a senior prank or an inside job?"

"Not officially. But I have a feeling we're dealing with seniors. A rookie down at the fire department went outside to dump the garbage and heard someone poking around their float. But they ran off before he spotted them. Thankfully also before they had a chance to do any damage."

Janet thought back to Tiffany's senior year, then her own. Some kids in her class had set a pig loose in the halls but never got caught. Tiffany came home with stories of funny additions to the morning announcements and the baseball coach waking up to a front lawn full of plastic forks. "Don't seniors usually pull pranks on campus or with specific teachers?"

"Usually. There's always that one outlier."

"Kim offered to let me, Debbie, and Paulette use one of the old repair garages at the depot to work on the café float. So if your outlier decides to make the rounds to other entries, ours will be safe in a locked garage."

"What do you ladies have cooked up? Pardon the pun. You never told me what came of your big meeting at Debbie's the other day."

"You'll see. To borrow a line from Harry, I can't have you stealing any ideas."

"I told you what the department is doing."

"But now that I know the floats are in danger of practical jokes, I'm feeling protective." In reality, she was just enjoying the game of taking the competition to the next level. Ranger curled up tighter on her lap and started purring. "See, Ranger agrees with me."

"What will you do if you need my help with something that requires power tools or heavy lifting? Make me do it blindfolded?"

She hadn't thought of that. At some point, the table would need to be bolted to the flatbed trailer that Debbie planned to borrow from Connor Construction. "Maybe. Or we can make you sign a nondisclosure agreement." She watched for Ian's response out of the corner of her eye. "You might also start planning for what you'll do if your team is working on the float during café hours and someone on your team has a craving for quality baked goods. We can't have you sending spies to our construction zone."

Ian put a throw pillow behind his head and leaned back. "I'll pay Tiffany to pick some up."

"Tiffany will be busy with games. She doesn't have time to be your errand girl." Janet let out a long sigh. "I guess you and your fellow officers will have to settle for convenience store pastries and bad coffee that day."

"I'd rather starve, thank you."

Teasing Ian resurrected a memory of catching up with Mandy. She and Gary always had a funny way of bantering without sounding angry. She let the wave of grief for her friend become a silent prayer for her and the girls.

"It was so nice to see Mandy doing well."

"It still disturbs me whenever I think about Gary having a heart attack. He ran marathons and ate healthier than anyone I knew."

Janet had forgotten all about the marathons. "It's so unsettling. He is a good reminder that we never know what the next moment holds."

"It makes me want to make the most of every day I have."

"Me too." And maybe seize more opportunities, like waiting lists for baking workshops. "Do you ever regret not traveling more? Outside our typical excursions to state parks and beach houses?" Since catching up with Mandy, the heartbreaking loss that allowed her friend the freedom to teach in London had gotten mingled with an intensifying regret over the study abroad that took Mandy away for a semester.

Ian adjusted the pillow behind his head. "What made you think of that?"

"Oh, you know how it is when we catch up with friends we haven't seen in a while." She and Ian had just talked about a friend's passing, and now she was drumming up travel remorse. But she couldn't exactly leave her story unfinished, so she told him all about it. "Mandy asked if I wanted to get on the wait list for the program she's teaching for in London."

"Wow."

"It got me thinking about when I was in college and Cleveland State offered a semester in Italy for fall of my junior year. Mandy went. She begged me to sign up. But when I thought about spending a whole semester on the other side of the Atlantic, I chickened out. I told her my parents couldn't afford it, which wasn't a lie. But I didn't even ask them. Now I wish I'd been less of a baby."

"I have regrets like that too. I'm pretty sure everyone has at least one."

"If Tiffany wanted to do a study abroad program, I would say yes in two seconds."

"So would I. 'Travel while you're young and have the freedom,' that's what I'd tell her." Ian moved the pillow to his lap. "But as far as regretting not traveling much as a family, I don't think it's as unusual as it feels to you right now. For us, it's always been hard to find a big chunk of time to get away. Now that we're talking about it, however, I would like to take you and Tiffany to Scotland someday." His brogue became more pronounced. "To see the land of my people."

"Tiffany would love it. We could plan ahead and start saving now. For next summer maybe?" If she couldn't change her choice about studying abroad, she could at least plan an adventure for the future.

"We could swing it with enough notice. I certainly have my share of unused vacation time. Let's start looking into it."

"That would be great."

"I never expected you to catch the travel bug. You've always been so content to be in your hometown."

"It's hard not to catch the bug after hearing about the two weeks Mandy spent in England, a chocolate making class in France, and her upcoming teaching engagement." Janet folded her arms behind her head and slumped down on the couch. Ranger stretched and jumped to the floor. "I guess I got envious." She put her feet on the coffee table.

"That settles it. We're making it happen. Next summer. Scotland. Two weeks."

Janet threw up her fists. "Yes!"

Laddie perked up his ears and sat erect in his dog bed.

"We'll see Edinburgh Castle, walk the Royal Mile, visit the Loch Ness Monster."

"Buy a set of bagpipes."

Ian wrinkled his nose.

"Maybe not the bagpipes."

Ian tossed the pillow aside. He whipped around. "I have an idea. If one of us wins the float contest, that person gets an extra fifty pounds of spending money in Scotland next year."

Janet held up her hand for a high five. "You're on."

After a busy Saturday at the café and creating a float prep and doughnut-making schedule with Debbie and Paulette, Janet welcomed a quiet Mother's Day with church and Tiffany's homecoming for the summer.

An hour after unloading her car and serving Janet a pizza lunch, complete with flowers, Tiffany started the expected load of laundry. Janet joined her in her childhood bedroom to help put away what she'd brought home.

"Are you excited to get started on game planning?"

"I already did some on Friday." Tiffany took the last pair of jeans out of her suitcase. "I planned to do nothing, which meant my mind started spinning with ideas." She zipped her suitcase and parked it in her closet. "Melissa Danner from the events committee encouraged me to form a team, so I asked Layla, and also Catherine Cartwright. They both said yes. The biggest challenge will be getting all the supplies. Greg sent me the budget and a list of online rental companies and catalogues for carnival games and prizes. I want to stretch it as much as possible."

"We can dig your old cornhole game out of the garage."

"I know you're kidding, but it might not be a bad idea. Who doesn't love cornhole? And it's one less thing to buy or rent."

"What games did you come up with during your veg-out day that turned into a brainstorming session?"

Tiffany opened her bottom dresser drawer and found a spot for her jeans. "So far, my list includes milk bottle toss, balloon darts, tossing rings over rubber ducks, and a fishing-for-prizes game. I'm also hoping to find Ring the Bell—the one where you whack a pivot with a mallet."

"Will any of the games be rigged like at a real carnival?"

Tiffany knelt in front of her dresser. "It's tempting to throw one in as a joke. Oh, and Lydia says we need to include a table-tennis ball toss for goldfish for sure. You can't have a carnival without goldfish as prizes."

Janet sank onto the edge of Tiffany's bed. "Your first pet was a carnival goldfish."

Tiffany slowly shut the bottom drawer. "I remember that fish. I named him Nemo." Her hands lingered on the drawer knobs. "I do believe he changed color one day while I was at kindergarten."

Ah, yes. The day Janet found her five-year-old's goldfish floating on the surface of the water and didn't feel ready to turn the experience into a talk about the reality of death. Instead, she'd driven to the pet store and found the closest match possible to dear Nemo. "What can I say? It's tough being a parent."

A buzzer announced the completion of Tiffany's first load of dry clothes. She hopped up with the energy reserved for the young.

She returned a moment later with a basket overflowing with clothes. She dumped the contents on her bed and started sorting. "I heard Jasmine Greene is in Dennison doing research."

"How did you know?"

"Her sister, Dalia, is a friend of mine. We kept ending up in fitness classes together and finally started planning to take the same ones to keep motivated. Full confession: We first connected when both of us almost got asked to leave an exercise class for the day for laughing."

Janet picked up two socks to fold them. She playfully swatted her daughter's arm with one of them. "Tiffany Arabella."

"I couldn't help it. The instructor was a guy and extremely dramatic." Tiffany lifted her arms overhead. "'Take your shoulders out of your ears.'" She slowly moved her fists to her hips and did a squat. "'Work from the inside out, not the outside in.'" She let her arms drop. "One day he said *sitz bones* one too many times, and we totally lost it."

Janet pictured an athletic dude in workout pants saying every line that came out of her daughter's mouth and burst out laughing. "Yeah, when did sitz bones become so important? I didn't know I had them until I tried out an online exercise course."

"Try hearing the term twenty times in one class session. That explains my B in the class during freshman year. At least it didn't keep me from making the Dean's List." She grabbed a T-shirt out of the pile.

Janet folded the pair of socks together and tossed them on the bed. "I probably would have, judging by my inability to hold it together just now." She noticed a black sock on the floor right outside Tiffany's bedroom door and another a few feet away from it. "You left a trail, my dear."

The words had barely left her mouth when Laddie came out of nowhere and grabbed one of the socks. He took off down the hall.

"Laddie!" Tiffany ran after him. When she caught up, she whisked him up long enough for a playful game of tug of war. She managed to loosen his grip on the sock. "You slimed it." She gave the dog a snuggle and set him down. She tossed the sock into her hamper on her way to the bed, Laddie at her heels. He made himself comfortable on a blanket in the corner of the room.

Tiffany wiped her hands over her jeans. "Now that I've admitted being naughty in class, this might not be the best time to make a request. But I'm pressed for time on planning games so—" She clasped her hands. "Will you please donate a cake to my cake walk? The events committee *really* wants a cake walk."

"A cake walk? Which decade are we living in?"

"1945." Tiffany tilted her head. "Please, Mom?"

"It's Mother's Day. I'm supposed to be asking you for favors."

Tiffany batted her eyes.

"Are you sure it wasn't a drama class that you almost got kicked out of for the day?"

She formed her mouth into a pitiful frown.

"I have to think about it, sweetie pie. I volunteered to make a hundred doughnuts to pass out from the café float."

"Oh. That's a lot." Tiffany took a blue top from her pile.

"Yeah. A lot, a lot."

Tiffany slapped on a cheesy grin. "But you love to bake. And you love me, your favorite daughter, even more."

"My only daughter."

"Exactly. Your *only* daughter."

Janet selected a pair of workout shorts from Tiffany's laundry pile. "Tell you what. Since I'm making doughnuts anyway, I'll add an extra dozen for the cake walk. Final offer."

"Yes! Thank you." Tiffany threw her arms around Janet. Then she continued folding the shirt and laid it aside. "So, back to Jasmine." Tiffany kicked off her shoes, crossed her legs on the bed, and resumed her folding. "Her sister was happy to see Jasmine apply for the longevity project. Apparently, she almost didn't."

Janet sat across from her daughter and folded a pair of black no-show socks. "Jasmine told me and Debbie that she begged to be part of the Dennison group."

"The possibility of going to Dennison was what finally motivated her to apply. Before that, Dalia was worried that Jasmine might give up on medical school."

"Why?"

"I'm not sure how much is public knowledge, so I'll try not to overshare. But what I can tell you is Jasmine got in a bad car accident over winter break. She hasn't been completely the same since."

"I never would have guessed. She seemed fine when she came into the café the other day."

"Dalia hasn't shared all the details, only that Jasmine struggled a lot even after she seemed fully recovered. Then her great-grand-father passed away, and that was hard for her. They had grown close after her accident."

No wonder she begged to be in a group that would bring her to her great-grandfather's hometown. "I'm glad she's here. Harry sure seemed eager to share stories with her. I hope her time in Dennison provides—I don't know—some healing."

"I hope so too."

On Monday morning, Debbie threw the kitchen doors open while Janet was whipping up an applesauce cake. She held the doors apart with her hands, her purse dangling from one elbow. "I tried your lasagna recipe Saturday night, and the brownie pudding. I've completely raised the bar on what my guys can expect to eat at home."

"I'm so glad."

"So that settles it. Starting tomorrow, I want to put your cookbook on display in the café so customers can buy copies of their own."

"Great!" Janet poured a jar of chunky applesauce into her batter and worked off the moment of panic with her giant wooden spoon. "I only made that one copy though."

"We can take orders with the first batch, which will include one for the café so I can have mine at home."

Janet predicted a sequel in her future. "Maybe we'll think of a charity to support with the profits."

"I can't think of one right at the moment, but for now we'll have fun watching it fly off the shelves." Debbie pulled off her jacket and hung it up. She rested her palms on the counter beside Janet. "This is totally off-topic, but Greg told me what happened to the Dennison Police Department's float. Ian mentioned it at church."

Once again, Janet visualized melting light bulbs and let out a snort. "People can be so immature."

"Did you laugh when Ian told you?"

"Oh, yeah."

"Do you think it's a sign of things to come? That the float contest is going to become a 'Who can pull the most childish prank' competition?"

"It could be. The fire department would've been the next targets if not for a rookie taking out the trash. Ian thinks we're dealing with senior pranks."

"Greg and I guessed the same. 'Tis the season."

Debbie left Janet to finish her applesauce cake. By opening time, the entire café smelled like apple heaven.

When Patricia came in for her morning mocha, she sniffed the air from the doorway to the counter. "Whatever I smell, I want some, please."

Janet handed Debbie an order of Wartime Potato Cakes. "It's almost cooled off," she told Patricia.

Twenty minutes later, Janet made a grand entrance into the dining room with a tray of applesauce cake in one hand and plated slice in the other. "Applesauce cake for Ms. Patricia Franklin."

Patricia set her mocha down. "Yay!"

Janet saw Harry sitting beside his granddaughter. "That looks tasty. I think I'll have the same, but ordinary coffee instead of the mocha."

Debbie returned from delivering more potato cakes and got Janet a plate for Harry's cake before she had to ask for one.

"So, Harry," Debbie asked him, "are you enjoying being part of the longevity study?"

Harry shrugged. "I kind of expected it to be more interesting." He picked up the fork beside his plate. "But it's a lot like going to the doctor for my yearly checkup. On the first day, they weighed us and took our vitals. We filled out questionnaires about our diet and exercise. They've asked about our support systems, family history, and whatnot. The only difference between Jasmine and Amber and my GP is, Jasmine and Amber also watch me, Ray, and Eileen hang out in the rec room and take notes. They take a lot of pictures and videos. Yesterday, Ray joked that he now knows how a lab rat feels."

Patricia took a bite of her cake and chewed it with her eyes closed. She pointed to Harry's plate with her fork and urged him to try his. "Maybe this is phase one and the project will get more exciting later."

"I hope so." Harry stuck his fork into his cake. "Jasmine and Amber are sweet girls. We like having them around. Jasmine and I have been able to share stories about her great-grandfather. He was blinded while fighting in the Pacific. I got to know him well when Sylvia and I invited him to help us with the float back in '46."

"Who knows?" Janet said. "Maybe you're supposed to be part of the project to connect with Jasmine."

"Maybe. If that's the case, I'm happy to participate."

Debbie filled a cup of coffee and set it in front of Harry. "What about your big float idea? Are you making progress on that?"

"Some. We might need to scale back a bit, unfortunately. Other than a few ladies who offered to help make decorations, Ray, Eileen, and I are the only ones who want to participate in the design process. We kind of underestimated what it took to create a float. We must be getting old."

Janet patted Harry's back. "You aren't old, Harry."

Debbie offered him a basket of creamers. "Don't give up on your dream just yet."

Whatever Harry's dream idea was, Janet so wanted to know. "I bet you can find someone to help you."

"If you know of anyone who wants to help out, we'd appreciate you pointing them our way."

Janet was replenishing the bakery case when Jasmine and Amber came into the café and took seats at the counter.

Jasmine hooked her tote bag over the back of her stool and walked to the bakery case. Her eyes seemed more tired than on the day she and Amber arrived in Dennison, ready to contribute great things to the world of geriatric research.

Amber took a covered clipboard out of her bag and laid it on the counter. She opened it, closed it again, and made eye contact with Janet. "Can Jasmine and I ask a favor?"

Janet straightened a row of snickerdoodles. "Ask away."

"Debbie might be able to help us too."

Tossing her towel aside, Debbie came over. Jasmine abandoned the bakery selection and returned to her place next to Amber.

Amber tucked her curls behind her ears. "We've run into a bit of a dead end with our project at Good Shepherd. Since you know our subjects better than we do, we thought you might be able to help us come up with ways to get them more relaxed and engaged."

"They are wonderful people. But today they seemed a bit—I don't know—" Jasmine looked over at Amber "—unenthusiastic."

The word *subjects* made Janet cringe. She managed to restrain herself from letting it show. At least Jasmine and Amber were aware their "subjects" were bored.

"Janet," Debbie whispered, "maybe this is the answer to Harry's problem."

Janet thought for a moment. "You're right." She set her empty cookie tray on the counter behind her. "I think Debbie and I have a solution."

Jasmine reached into her tote and pulled out a similar covered clipboard, except hers was blue and Amber's was red. She flipped it open.

Janet tried hard not to give away how amusing the young women looked with their clipboards. They had gone into full-on researcher mode. No wonder Ray and Harry felt like specimens. "You can go ahead and put the clipboards away for this."

Amber gazed down at her folder like she wasn't sure she knew how to listen to project suggestions without taking notes. Jasmine moved hers aside.

Janet leaned against the counter in an attempt to encourage Jasmine and Amber to revert to the relaxed version of themselves. "I'm not sure if I mentioned this the other day, but Harry, Ray, and Eileen are some of Dennison's most beloved citizens. Besides their obvious longevity, they've led full and interesting lives. Harry is a great example. He started working at the depot as a porter at age fifteen and went on to become the conductor. He was here during World War II when soldiers from the troop trains stopped in Dennison before heading overseas. Eileen worked at the depot to support her father, who'd come home from World War I injured. She took over the role of stationmaster at twenty when all the adult men at the station went off to war."

Jasmine mouthed *Wow.* "So, by the time she was our age, she had already been running this depot for two years?"

"That's right. It still blows my mind when I think about how young some of my friends were during the war. Ray signed up for the army on his eighteenth birthday. He fought in Holland and the British Isles and came home injured."

Amber leaned back in her stool. "My brother is eighteen. They were kids."

Debbie brought over two glasses of iced tea. "The house you're staying in used to belong to Ray Zink. He lived in it until a couple of years ago." She went to grab some menus. "They are perfect reminders that elderly men and women are more than their age. They were once children, teenagers, young adults. I don't think of Harry as a man in his nineties when he comes into the café each morning. I think of him as my friend. Someone I hope to be more like when I grow up."

Janet pushed the sugar over in case the girls wanted to sweeten their tea. "So here's an idea. What if you were to take a break from the health and wellness questions and get to know those in your focus group as people? Hang out with them. Exchange stories. Find out what they do for fun. Ask Harry and Eileen about what it was like working at the depot when it became famous for its Salvation Army Canteen. Notice what makes them laugh, what makes them sad. Find things you have in common. After all, when you have your own patients, they will want to be treated as people, not subjects or case studies or slots in your schedule."

Debbie set the two menus down and fanned them out. "You might discover that the secret to their longevity is about more than good habits."

Jasmine took a menu. "Just sitting here talking to you shows me that they have a wonderful support system. Not everyone has that."

Amber took a couple sips of her iced tea. She opened her folder and jotted down a note. "Do you have any suggestions for activities?"

Janet filled a glass of water for herself and offered one to Debbie. "I happen to know that Harry, Eileen, and Ray would love some help with a float they're planning for the Memorial Day celebration. Harry has an idea, and today I could tell he was disappointed over not being able to make it happen."

A wistfulness filled Jasmine's eyes. "It would make me so happy to do that for him. Harry told me today that my great-grandfather helped him with a float after the war. This would feel like a tribute to Great-Grandpa. What does Harry have in mind?"

Janet threw up her hands. "He won't tell us."

Amber laughed. "That sounds like Harry."

"So in addition to forming relationships that give your project a personal touch, you'll be privy to inside information."

A threesome of women came in. Debbie hurried over to greet them then came back. "You girls can provide the youthful energy and lifting abilities they need to make the picture in Harry's mind a reality."

Janet suddenly recalled a kid in the biology class she slogged her way through in college. He was struggling to pass and did a video presentation about his physical therapy after a knee injury and got an A. "Instead of data charts and graphs, you can take pictures and film the group doing something relatable. Wouldn't showing them in action make for a more engaging presentation than simply saying, 'They're active'?"

Amber clicked her pen. "We do have lots of graphs."

Jasmine leaned her elbow on the counter. "And let's face it. Anyone can create them."

Janet loved hearing a smart premed student admit that graphs were lame.

Amber turned her stool to face Jasmine. "I haven't heard of anyone taking this approach to a graduate project. Not in our cohort anyway."

Jasmine scribbled on her clipboard. "We have their medical information, family history, and lifestyle habits. What does that really tell us?"

Amber shut her folder and slapped the top of it. "Let's do it."

Janet prepared to gather her things and do the next task on her list for the day: Buy freezer bags for the Memorial Day doughnuts. "You will make some dear friends extremely happy."

Jasmine dropped her clipboard into her tote. "Now I'm excited to go the Good Shepherd tomorrow. I can't wait to find out what Harry has in mind for the float."

Janet started toward the kitchen. "We're pretty eager to find out too."

CHAPTER EIGHT

The next morning, Janet enjoyed the quiet of the café kitchen while mixing jelly roll cake batter for that day's Homefront Bakery special. She carefully laid the warm cake over a clean dish towel and started rolling it to cool before making a second cake. In the first week of offering World War II-era specials, the Homefront Bakery offerings always went quickly. She and Debbie had determined that wartime foods were fun when neither those eating the goodies nor those preparing them had to ration their flour and sugar. She would reserve a few slices for samples. The carrot cake samples had been a smash. For everyone except Tristan Eger.

Janet paused for a moment to do a quick inventory of ingredients she'd set aside for baking sugar cookies with the field trip group from Claymont Elementary School.

"Flour, sugar, baking powder, shortening…" She named each item right down to kid-sized paper aprons. Finally, she could continue with the jelly rolls.

She went to her tote bag for a jar of raspberry jam from home. She heard the café door open and checked her watch. It seemed a little early for Debbie to come in, but it couldn't be anyone else. Janet shouted "Hello!" and took her jam to the work area.

Debbie came into the kitchen with her wedding gift cookbook under her arm. "Morning." She tossed her tote bag on the floor. Her voice didn't hold the happily married tone it had since her wedding day.

Janet set the jam aside. "You okay?"

"Physically, I'm fine. Frustration level?" She swept her arms up as far as she could reach and let them fall to her thighs with a smack. "Not so much."

Janet added oil to the mixer bowl for her second jelly roll. "What happened?" She cracked the first egg.

"Last night, Greg and the boys went to the construction office to work on their float and discovered it had been vandalized."

"No!" Janet said. It was time to take these pranks seriously. She cracked another egg.

"Yep." Debbie pulled over a stool and sank onto it with the cookbook in her lap. "Julian and Jaxon had spent a whole evening selecting plants and buying potting mix to use for their victory garden while Greg figured out how to create a planter box on his flatbed trailer. Then last night they filled a bunch of mason jars with soil to put some of the plants in as a nod to Greg's grandmother's canning classes. They left for one hour to get something to eat. When they went back, they found the mason jars emptied and potting mix spread all over the flatbed and inside Greg's truck."

"That's terrible." At least with headlights, the novelty bulbs could be replaced with ordinary ones. "Who would do that?"

"Who knows? The plants are fine, and very little potting mix got wasted. But the guys did not appreciate spending the rest of the night sweeping up soil, cleaning out the truck bed, and refilling the jars. Greg was not happy. It means someone was in the back parking lot of Connor Construction after he left. He felt perfectly safe leaving the plants and supplies overnight. Now he's figuring out a better solution."

Janet cracked the last of her eggs and added them to the mixer. "So now we know the infamous melting light bulbs on the Dennison Police float really were a sign of things to come."

"This didn't feel like a joke to Greg and the boys. It felt like someone purposely trying to set them back."

"I'm so sorry." Janet considered the theory of senior pranks. When students were responsible, their antics were rarely random.

"When I made that comment about this being a sign of things to come, I didn't expect it to actually happen." Debbie let out a growl. "We can't do anything about it now but rant and speculate. I came in early so I could do exactly that with you."

"If seniors are responsible, my first question would be if Jaxon had a conflict with any older students. But that wouldn't explain the Dennison Police float or the fire department."

Debbie got her phone and started typing at lightning speed.

"Are you texting Jaxon just in case?"

"No, I'm looking up common senior pranks." Debbie turned her screen around. "Make that epic senior pranks, according to what I see here."

"Do share." Janet slid her cake into the oven, set the timer, and pulled up another stool.

"Filling the hallway with helium balloons, letting crickets loose in a classroom, turning the cafeteria into a beach scene."

"That's actually a cute idea."

Debbie let out a loud laugh. "Okay, this one's funny. 'Have all the seniors bring alarm clocks to school and set them to go off at different times.'"

Janet pictured that happening with her most uptight high school teacher and started howling. She grabbed a paper towel to wipe away tears of laughter. "Nothing on this list is malicious."

"I can't leave this one out. 'Have the entire senior class break into the same song or dance at a specific time, no matter where they are.'" Debbie swiped the article closed. "The rest are equally as silly. I'll send you the article later."

Janet balled up her paper towel. It was smeared with mascara. "I don't think we're dealing with seniors."

"I did see a prank on the list that involves googly eyes. That's kind of similar to the melting light bulbs."

"It is. But why put melting light bulbs on the police department's float instead of somewhere on campus?"

Once the café opened, Janet set aside her thoughts on who was tampering with floats to serve up plenty of cornmeal pancake breakfast specials. She made it out to the counter just long enough to hear Debbie vent frustrations to Harry and Patricia over what happened to her favorite guys' float. Janet stayed so busy cooking breakfasts and prepping potatoes, onions, and cut-up hot dogs for the lunch special—poor man's meal, compliments of a suggestion from Harry—that she didn't have a minute to get in on the conversations.

Before Janet knew it, she was changing into her gingham apron with the cute baked goods on the pockets for the lunch rush. Janet finished tying her apron in back while nudging the kitchen door open. She found Debbie showing her cookbook off to Kim.

Kim moved to a stool with the book while Debbie adjusted the wooden stand she'd put on top of the bakery case. Kim turned one page then another. "Janet, you put this together? It's beautiful. I want one."

"Thank you." Even knowing she'd compiled the recipes hoping to eventually sell the book in the café, Janet found herself blushing over Kim's response to it.

Debbie pulled a pen out of her apron and set it on a homemade sign-up form beside the book stand. "You can request your copy here."

"I'll take two." Kim handed the cookbook back to Debbie and grabbed the pen. "One for myself and one to gift."

Janet watched Debbie move the cookbook to the center of the bakery case as if it were a bestseller by the latest celebrity chef. Paulette arrived as Kim was paying Debbie in cash for the copies while selling a customer on one as well.

Paulette put her arm around Janet's shoulders. "I already told Debbie to put me down for three, so I can set two aside for Christmas presents." She clapped her hands together. "You're going to be famous."

"Well, I don't know about famous. But it sure was a fun project."

Janet was about to head back to the kitchen when she saw Mandy beside the register counter. "Oh, hello there." She called Mandy over. "Debbie, Paulette, Kim, this is my friend Mandy. We went to college together."

Debbie took an envelope out of her pocket and slid Kim's book payment inside. "It's nice to finally meet the famous Mandy."

"Nice to finally meet you." Mandy exchanged hellos with Paulette and Kim. After Kim excused herself to get back to work at the museum, Mandy made her way over to the bakery case. "Do I see a cookbook with your name on it, Janet?"

Janet took the book off its stand and gave it to Mandy. "I made it as a wedding gift for Debbie."

"Which," Debbie added, "we're now selling copies of because it's that incredible."

"Yum." Mandy traced a finger over the cover. "I don't want to interrupt. I've been wanting to see the café, so I came in for a late breakfast slash early lunch during my break." She glanced over at the specials board. "I think I'll see how the poor man's meal tastes. Is it okay if I look through Janet's cookbook while I wait?"

"Of course." Debbie folded the stand and laid it on top of her order form.

A party of six moms with little ones put an end to the visit.

Janet went to work on Mandy's meal while Paulette collected orders from the party of moms. When Janet personally delivered Mandy's food, she found her chatting with Debbie and comparing childhood favorites from the *Cookies* section of her cookbook.

Once the tableful of mothers had their salads, drinks, and kids' meals, the pace in the kitchen slowed down. Janet ventured out to the dining room and saw Mandy still at the table, with her empty plate pushed to the side and her laptop open. The cookbook was back in its place.

Debbie met her at the counter with an armload of dirty dishes. "Take advantage of the pause and visit with Mandy for a while. Paulette and I can handle things."

"Thank you. I'll take you up on that." Janet poured a cup of coffee and wandered over. "It was so nice of you to wait."

"I figured I couldn't come down here and not at least try to wait for you to be free." Mandy shut her laptop and moved it aside. "I enjoyed looking through your cookbook."

Janet sat across from Mandy and doctored up her black coffee with creamer. "I must confess it is so encouraging to see everyone's response to it. I didn't think I would ever finish."

Mandy put her laptop into her tote bag. "You did a great job with it. Take it from a woman who found herself in charge of a church cookbook." She pointed to herself. "Have you ever thought about teaching cooking classes?"

"I've done some teaching in the community and liked it a lot. But the café keeps me busy." Janet stirred her coffee and took a sip. "The nice thing about that cookbook was I got to do it in my spare time."

"I certainly understand that. When Gary and I ran our restaurant, I felt like it owned us."

"Thankfully, I can't say the café owns me. We're only open for breakfast and lunch, and we close on Sundays." Not many restaurant owners had a guaranteed weekend day off and evenings free. "I feel like I have my dream job co-owning this place with Debbie. I get to see regulars every day and keep up with what's going on without turning on the news. The locals have become like family."

"No wonder you've stayed close to home. Every workday includes hanging out with your friends."

"That's exactly what it's like."

"Well, if you ever find you need to make a change, I highly recommend teaching based on what I saw in that book."

"Thank you. That means a lot to me. Especially coming from someone who hit the baking school big time."

Janet couldn't imagine a better compliment than that.

Ian hadn't even put his key fob on the kitchen counter when Janet turned away from her boiling pot of spaghetti noodles and simmering meat sauce to tell him. "You will not believe what Debbie told me."

"I heard. Greg came into the station to file a report, so we'll have it on record."

"So now you can't brush off what happened to your float as a joke."

"I guess I can stop interrogating members of the department who aren't on the float committee and start in on every high school senior I pass on the street."

Janet turned down the temperature on the water. She told him about the list of senior pranks Debbie pulled up, and the conclusion it led them to. "This doesn't line up with what we read."

"You have a good point. In addition to the incidents happening off campus, seniors usually leave some kind of message that gives them away."

"Right, like their graduation year in tealight candles." Janet gazed up at the ceiling, thinking. "Funny that whoever is doing this chose your float, Greg's, and almost the fire department's, but not ours. I'm sure it's because this vandal holds a special place in their heart for the café. I bet they want our float to win." Never mind that she, Debbie, and Paulette didn't have much to mess with yet except a painted wooden table.

Ian took a spoon out of the utensil drawer. He lifted the lid off the sauce. "Either that or they're saving the best for last." He dipped in his spoon. "You'll hand out your doughnuts during the parade and discover they've been replaced with slime doughnuts that ooze all over as soon as the heat of human hands touch them. All the children will cry, and you'll be disqualified."

"Don't ever repeat that in public. Whoever dumped potting mix all over Greg's flatbed might hear you."

CHAPTER NINE

Dennison, Ohio
May 11, 1946

Even though Saturday was always a busy day at the depot, Harry seized every free moment during his shift to check in with Sylvia while she and Bradley started the troop car. Miss Eileen had found them a perfect spot in the area usually designated for repairing trains. Having Bradley involved had drawn Mitch in for an extra set of hands.

Miss Eileen came over as Harry was helping Sylvia drag a long slab of siding to the outside wall of the maintenance shed.

Bradley watched from the sidelines. His eyes pinched with the strain it took to see as much as possible with his one partially functional eye. "I'm picturing three windows on each side of the car."

Eileen stood beside Bradley. She cocked her head to the left. "The only thing missing from our troop car is passengers."

Harry caught himself wishing that Bradley had enough eyesight to paint a face in each window. Even cartoony images would add to the joy of a float welcoming troops home.

Sylvia paced in front of the siding. "We could ask Mitch and some other station employees to act as passengers, but it wouldn't be the same as having real soldiers."

"And they wouldn't be in uniform," Bradley pointed out.

Sylvia walked up to the siding slab and held her hands up like a frame. She dropped her arms, one hand landing firm on her waist. "We can't have empty windows."

Harry considered the many veterans who'd returned to Dennison since the war ended. Ray Zink, Sylvia's father and uncle, her brother, James. Each branch of the military, as well as the VA, had been asked to march in the parade, but maybe they could borrow a few men. "How about asking some of the veterans to ride on our float?"

Bradley cleared his throat. "I know of some who aren't marching in the parade with the others. One young man who lost his right leg and another who has a permanent limp declined the invitation. Two who require wheelchairs now did as well. They said they don't want to slow everyone down."

Miss Eileen's face clouded over with sadness that Harry knew flowed from years of supporting her father. "Surely someone can help them along."

"I don't think they want to draw attention, Miss Eileen. These are men who were able-bodied when they left for Europe or the Pacific, fought hard, and came home needing to relearn how to do everyday things. And learn how to rely on others for help. It's hard for them."

Harry's mental picture of painted cartoon faces switched to a much more personal one that included men who would otherwise be on the sidelines or stay home. "If they ride on our float, no one will see their injuries."

Sylvia touched Bradley's shoulder. "Bradley, will you invite them? Tell your friends how much we need their help. That the float won't be the same without them."

Harry saw Bradley's chin start to tremble a little. Bradley turned away. He regained his composure. "You have no idea what it will mean to them to know how much you want them involved, and in a way where they won't feel like everyone is watching them with pity."

Miss Eileen put a hand on Bradley's shoulder. "If you still have spaces to fill after asking your friends, I'm sure my dad would be happy to ride on our float. His bum leg makes marching in parades challenging."

When Harry pictured their completed float, only one thing complicated the plan. "We'll need a ramp to get the two in wheelchairs onto the back of the truck, right?"

"We'll build one." Sylvia's answer came so quickly that Harry realized she'd been one step ahead.

The emotions that swept over Bradley's face a moment before brightened into winsomeness. "Would it be silly to have them throw candy to the crowd?"

Miss Eileen checked her watch and dropped it back into her pocket. "I don't think so. Why not throw candy? We're commemorating the end of a long war, and those who fought in it. Let's make our float the most festive in the parade. In fact, I'll volunteer to buy a bunch of penny candy and see if Rafe wants to contribute as well."

Sylvia kept her eyes on the siding as if already imagining candy flying from windows they were yet to create. "I'll buy some too."

"So will I." Harry didn't even have think about it. After all the men sacrificed, the least he could do was set aside some of his paycheck for a bag of bubble gum and taffy.

"And I'll reach out to the guys starting today." Bradley wrapped his hands around the handle of his cane like he planned to go right way. "Thank you for making me part of this. I'm having a great time, and we haven't even started building yet. It feels good to do something artistic again, even if I'm only passing on the ideas in my head."

Miss Eileen looked over at Sylvia then at Harry. "This seems like a fitting time for the two of you to tell Bradley about the idea you came up with. I need to get back to the depot, so I'll leave you to it."

Harry nodded to Sylvia, who immediately took off in the direction of the repair shed where Bradley had fixed his brother's bike the day before. Harry put his hand on Bradley's arm. "Follow me. Sylvia and I have a job for you."

"What sort of job?"

"You'll see."

Harry looked over his shoulder just long enough to see a boyish anticipation build on Bradley's face. Bradley's excitement was so contagious that Harry almost broke out into a run. When he reached the shed, Sylvia was waiting in the doorway.

She pushed the door open with her back and swept her arm to the inside. "Enter, gentlemen."

"After you, Bradley." Harry made room for Bradley to enter the shed ahead of him. His heart started racing with eagerness.

Harry retrieved the lantern from the corner and brought it to the worktable. "I found this lantern when you were fixing Mitch's bike."

Sylvia recapped their vision for the float's focal point, right down to the flowers and flowing ribbons they would add once Bradley finished his part. "So, are you interested?"

Bradley stepped past Sylvia and took hold of the lantern. He wrapped his fingers around the handle and placed his other hand under the base. He explored every inch of the surface with his hands. He set it down again.

Harry's heart sank. Maybe it was beyond repair.

Bradley leaned in close, favoring the eye that still had some vision. "Is Miss Eileen okay with me using this?"

Sylvia inched her way to the side of the worktable and reached behind it. "She gave the go-ahead yesterday."

Bradley kept hold of the lantern. He wiggled the handle back and forth. It squeaked like an old gate.

Harry struggled to read what might be going on in Bradley's mind.

Bradley smiled. "I think I know what I want to do. I'll bring my tools over tomorrow."

"I was hoping you'd say that." Sylvia pulled out a wooden plank with a piece of rope attached to each top corner. She held it behind her back until she was right in front of Bradley. "Hold your hands out."

Bradley let go of the lantern and put both hands out. "What are you up to?"

Sylvia hung the rope over Bradley's palms. "I know artists don't like to be bothered while they're working, so I made you a privacy sign. It says 'Artist at Work. Do Not Disturb.'" She put her hands in the back pockets of her jeans. "I painted the letters thick, so you'd be able to feel them and know which side to face out."

Harry thumped the shed door. "I put a nail up for you to hang the sign on."

"I don't know what to say." Bradley took hold of the edges of the sign and turned it around. "I've always dreamed of being commissioned as an artist."

He'd given up on that dream. Harry knew it without Bradley having to say so. The bittersweet expression said it all.

A woman's voice came from outside. "Bradley?"

He turned toward the sound. "That's Margo. I didn't know she was coming to see me."

Sylvia ran for the door.

"Wait." Bradley put his finger over his lips. "Let's make this a surprise for the community."

Sylvia whispered, "Yes." Her whole face beamed over the mention of a secret.

Harry frantically looked for something to cover the lantern and sign. He found an old drop cloth and draped it over the worktable.

Sylvia opened the door. "Hi, Margo."

Margo stood outside in her nursing uniform. She gave a little wave. "Surprise."

Harry watched as Bradley's expression transformed from stunned to full of soft affection for the young woman in front of him. Bradley held out his hand. Margo took it. They exchanged wordless greetings that reflected Harry's own feelings for Sylvia. At that moment, Harry recognized that while Bradley's sight had been taken from him, the part of him that adored Margo would never change.

"Surprise yourself," Bradley said in a way that showed he was glad she dropped by unannounced.

"You came to walk me home at the end of my shift the other day, so I thought I'd do the same for you." Margo said hello to Harry and Sylvia. "Am I interrupting something important?"

"We were planning a design for the float." Bradley reached beside the shed door where he'd leaned his cane.

Harry closed the shed. "We're finished for today. How about if we meet again tomorrow after church to start assembling?"

Bradley said, "I'll add that to my busy social calendar."

Margo gently laid her hand on Bradley's arm and held out her elbow. Bradley took hold of it without her having to offer in words. They waved goodbye to Harry in unison and walked away.

Harry overheard Margo's words to Bradley. "I saw a poster for The Postman Always Rings Twice in front of the movie theater. Do you want to go after supper tonight?"

"Last time we went to the pictures the couple behind us got mad when you described what was going on."

"I'll be quieter this time."

"Okay. It's a date."

Sylvia flashed another glowing smile. "They are such a sweet couple. I'm glad Bradley is part of our team."

Harry watched the two make their way down the road. Bradley looked so at ease holding Margo's arm. "It's all thanks to you."

Bradley and Margo fit. He couldn't imagine anything coming between them.

CHAPTER TEN

anet had just served Patricia a slice of cinnamon bread to go with her Wednesday morning peppermint mocha when Jim Watson from the *Gazette* came into the café. He had a laptop case slung over one shoulder and the stride of a confident newspaper editor. Jim said hello to Janet and Patricia and picked up a menu.

Debbie met him near the register. "Morning, Jim. Do you want to sit, or are you getting something to go?"

Jim flipped to the breakfast page. "I'd like something to go this time. I have a busy day ahead. One of my writers is due to turn in a piece covering what's been going on with the floats, and I want to get it up on the website as soon as it arrives in my inbox."

In the day since Debbie told Janet about what happened to the Connor Construction float, word had gotten around. Half of Janet's conversations with customers included concern about floats. A writer from the *Gazette* had called Ian the night before to ask about possible safety concerns.

Janet gave Patricia a pat of butter for her cinnamon bread. "Jim, if you want something hearty, we have a Victory Garden Scramble, with cheese or without. It comes with country potatoes and toast."

"That sounds good." He returned his menu to the stack. "I'll have mine with cheese and sourdough toast, and a large coffee, please."

"Good choice."

Janet pivoted to the kitchen and got right to work sautéing onions, mushrooms, bell peppers, and spinach for Jim's scramble. She recalled Ian's phone interview from the night before, his request that the article include a note to call the Dennison Police Department if they need to report float vandalism, and how he added, "Please don't call 911."

Tiffany'd had a remark for that. "Only in Dennison would 'A sign is missing from my float' be considered alarming enough to warrant a 911 call."

Janet told herself to focus on Jim's scramble and leave all concerns about float sabotage alone. Now that senior pranks seemed to be off the table, she and Debbie were at a loss for new suspects. *A local with a float in the competition maybe?* That would make the most logical sense. But who?

Two slices of sourdough popped out of the toaster. Janet cut them in half and slipped them into a small to-go bag so they wouldn't get soggy beside the scramble and potatoes. She walked the order out to Jim and found him seated beside Patricia at the counter.

"I can smell my omelet through the bag. It might not make it to my desk." Jim got up from his stool and took the box from Janet. "It sounds like we'll have a great lineup of floats for the parade."

Debbie slipped Jim's cup into a cardboard sleeve. "According to Greg, Pastor Nick entered one for Faith Community Church. The library is doing a float. Every local sport, dance studio, scout troop, and martial art studio signed up. The event committee asked Greg to add a 'Sorry, we're full' announcement to the parade page, unless we want to be watching Memorial Day floats until the Fourth of July."

Patricia crumpled her napkin. "Is the *Gazette* entering a float?"

"We sure are. I searched the archives for the *Gazette's* front pages for VE Day and VJ Day. They're at the printers as we speak, getting blown up large enough to be seen from the sidelines. One of our interns is going to play the part of a newsboy announcing the end of the war."

Patricia dropped her crumpled napkin on her plate and took her wallet out of her purse. "What a cool idea. I'm helping Charla Whipple sell food at the snack bar."

"You'll be seeing a lot of me then. One random fact about me is I have a weakness for carnival food." Jim took a handful of napkins from the dispenser. "Before I go, I need to show you all what else I found in the files from after the war." Jim set down his to-go container and opened his laptop case. From the middle pocket, he pulled a newspaper page covered in protective plastic. He laid it on the counter. "It's from 1946, when Dennison held an Honor Parade and Picnic."

Patricia took another napkin and wiped her fingers. "May I take a closer look at that? Pop Pop has been talking about the honor parade a lot lately."

Jim moved the article closer to Patricia then stepped aside and took out his credit card to pay for his breakfast. Janet followed Debbie to the other side of the counter and peered over her shoulder at the grainy collage of images. One picture showed locals standing along the parade route, holding American flags and noisemakers. In another, army veterans marched and waved.

Debbie pointed out a young man in uniform behind a truck with a group of other veterans, most around Tiffany's age. "Look, there's Ray."

Janet zeroed in on the largest photo in the spread, featuring a pickup truck transformed to resemble a passenger car from a train. A young Harry Franklin and a pretty woman who Janet recognized as his late wife, Sylvia, carried a sign that Janet couldn't quite make out. Men in uniform waved from the windows of the makeshift train. Some appeared to be tossing candy to the crowd. A little girl in a plaid jumper knelt to get a piece.

Debbie tapped the page with her index finger. "There's Eileen in front of Harry and Sylvia."

Janet leaned in for a better look. There Eileen marched, all smiles in her stationmaster uniform, holding a decorated railroad lantern, high and proud. The image was a bit fuzzy, but the ribbons streaming down the back of the lantern hinted at how lovely that lantern must have been in 1946.

Janet read the caption below the photo aloud for everyone. "The Dennison Depot stole the show with its 'Welcome Home' troop train, candy for the kids, and an ornate stationmaster lantern renovated by an anonymous craftsman." She got out of the way so Debbie could have a turn. "That must be the float Harry told us about last week. He failed to mention that it stole the show and ended up in the paper."

Janet returned for another look at Harry as an eighteen-year-old man and the woman who became his wife. Eileen in her youth, before she married her husband, Rafe Palmer, still overseeing the Dennison Depot. "Is the paper going to republish this? Locals will love to see it."

"It's going out on Sunday, in print and online. It'll be part of an article about our Memorial Day celebration. Hopefully, we've seen the last of the float nonsense, so we can keep the article celebratory."

Patricia got up from her stool. "I wonder if someone can locate that lantern. Wouldn't it be fun to have it on display on Memorial Day?"

Debbie took Jim's credit card. "I'll mention it to Greg. Someone in the chamber of commerce might know where to find it."

Janet handed the article back to Jim. "Or Kim might know."

Janet saw Harry coming into the café. "Jim, don't put the article away just yet." She rushed over to meet Harry. "I'm so glad you arrived before Jim left."

Patricia returned to her stool. "Come look at what Jim found in the archives."

Harry gave Crosby's leash a gentle tug. "Come on, Crosby, let's check it out." He claimed the stool beside his granddaughter's. He picked up the clipping then laid it carefully on the counter again, his face appearing lost in time. "There's my Sylvia." A melancholy smile spread across his lips. "I know it's not very creative to say I remember this parade like it was yesterday, but I really do. Sylvia, Eileen, and I created that float with Bradley Macomb—Jasmine's great-grandfather—and his brother Mitch. Sylvia managed the whole project. She was always talented that way. Even when we were married, she was handier around the house than me."

Janet pointed out the lantern. "Is she the one who made this?"

"No, no. But she's the reason we found the artist. That's a long story for another time."

Patricia moved closer to Harry looking like the little girl in her wanted to beg her grandpa to tell the story now. "I wish someone had taken a closeup of that lantern. From the way Eileen is carrying it, I get the impression it was special."

"It was something to see. I can tell you that." Harry handed the sheet to Jim.

Jim took another look at the old article. "I bet someone at the paper can zoom in and crop it for Sunday's article. Though it might not do the piece justice with such an old photo." Jim slid it into his case as if protecting a rare historical document. "Harry, do you happen to have an idea where the lantern might be now?"

Patricia checked her watch and hurried over to the register. "If you can find it, maybe you can add it to your float."

Harry got up from the stool. "That's what I was hoping for. That lantern hung in the depot for almost a year after the parade, until Eileen married Rafe and a new stationmaster took over. The other day, I asked Kim if she ever saw it anywhere, but she didn't recognize the lantern at all." Harry took a seat at the table nearest the counter. "It's a shame. If I'd known someone planned to get rid of it, I would've asked to take it home as a memory."

An image formed in Janet's mind of Eileen marching with the ribbon- and flower-adorned lantern, the same lantern hanging in a place of honor in the depot, and Harry finding it gone. Even now, his sadness over the loss showed in his countenance. It was a reminder of how each person who found their hard work tampered with must have felt, and why they needed to prevent similar incidents.

Janet was mulling over the long list of float contestants who could become suspects when Paulette arrived to help with the lunch rush.

Janet did a quick text check on her phone and saw a message from Tiffany with an attached picture of six aluminum bottles and a can of tennis balls.

One more game complete! Thank you, thrift stores.

Janet texted back, Woo-hoo!

We had to scrap the goldfish game. It'll cost too much.

Janet found the crying emoji for her reply.

Paulette took a daisy-print granny apron off its hook. "Greg told me the *Gazette* reached out to him with questions about his float incident."

Janet took a loaf of sourdough bread out of the pantry and dropped it on the counter. "They called Ian too."

"I'm wondering if they should title the article, 'Someone in Dennison Has Too Much Time on Their Hands.' Why do people have to ruin the fun by doing things like this?"

"Maybe it's someone desperate to win."

"I hope not. Everyone I know who entered a float sees it as a friendly competition, not a reason to sabotage neighbors."

"Thankfully, in a town the size of Dennison, if this person strikes again, their chance of getting caught goes up daily." Janet untwisted the tie on the bread bag.

Her phone dinged again.

"Sounds like Tiffany scored another carnival game." She tossed aside the twist tie and tapped the screen. Mandy's number appeared instead of Tiffany's. With everything prepped for the lunch rush, she tapped on it.

Hey friend! Do you have time to chat later today?

Janet considered her schedule for the afternoon. She'd planned to make a batch of doughnuts after the café closed so she could freeze them.

Sure. Come by the café after your class. I'll be here baking for the parade.

The ping of Mandy's reply was almost instantaneous. Perfect. See you soon.

Janet slipped her phone into her apron pocket. "Huh. I wonder what that's about."

Janet was sliding the last of that day's mini doughnuts onto the cooling rack when Mandy shouted hello from the dining room. Janet turned off the hot oil. "Coming!" She grabbed a damp towel for her hands and pushed her way through the double doors.

Mandy's smile brought up memories of the day she'd told Janet her parents said yes to the semester abroad program. She dropped her purse on the counter. "Hello again."

"Two days in a row. What a treat. Let me just take off my apron." Janet took a moment to make sure the oven was off. When she went back out, Mandy was sitting on one of the counter stools as if she'd lived in Dennison her whole life.

"Do you want to talk here or go someplace else? We have some leftover iced tea in the fridge."

Mandy surveyed the empty dining room. "Let's go someplace else."

"How about a walk?" Janet studied Mandy's face. She looked about to burst with something exciting.

"A walk sounds lovely. It's gorgeous outside. You can give me a personal tour of the station."

"All righty then. Let's go. You can stash your purse in the kitchen so you don't have to lug it around." Janet pushed the kitchen door open for Mandy to go in. "I'll lock the door on the way out. We can't be too careful these days."

"Thank you." Mandy gave Janet a confused look. "I thought Dennison was one of those towns where no one locks their door."

Janet led the way out of the café and into the waiting area. "Usually. Unless someone, say, decided to start vandalizing parade floats." Janet directed Mandy across the historic platform. "Thousands of World War II troop trains came through here, and volunteers kept the Salvation Army Canteen going around the clock. That's the café, now."

Mandy looked out toward the tracks where a historic train sat ready for tourists. "What's it like to spend every day in such a significant place?"

"Honestly, as a kid, I didn't think about it much. Even on the Fourth of July, I thought the fireworks were for my birthday. But since Debbie and I opened the café, I've grown to appreciate Dennison's history in a new way. I mean, think about the thousands of servicemen who walked along this platform." Janet stopped. Some, like Ray Zink, had come home. Others had not. "I love knowing this station is remembered for its hospitality."

Mandy rested both hands on the platform rail. "If you'd lived during World War II, I bet you would've cheered up countless soldiers with your cookies and cakes."

"I would've blown through my sugar rations in no time." Janet weighed the best places for her and Mandy to walk and talk. "Let me show you the Pullman. Kim Smith, our museum curator, turned an old railroad coach into a bed and breakfast. The first car was so popular that she purchased a second." Janet bounded down the steps. "One is in use and the other is most likely locked, but you can at least see the outside."

Mandy strolled beside Janet. "What a clever idea, turning rail cars into a bed and breakfast."

"Dennison isn't the tourism capital of the world, but we draw our share of families who enjoy taking their kids to historical sites during the summer." She glanced over at Mandy. "So, what do you want to chat about? Is everything going well with your class?"

"It's going extremely well." Mandy stopped in front of the original pullman car. "I'll cut right to the chase, so you don't think I'm about to deliver bad news."

"You look way too happy for that."

Mandy took hold of Janet's wrist and pulled her toward the small gate between the Pullman cars and the main train station. "You will not believe God's timing. Remember yesterday when I encouraged you to do more teaching?"

"Yeah."

"Well, last night, I got an email from my friend Glenis. One of the other guest instructors had to back out because of a health issue. Glenis had two alternates waiting in the wings, but both had to pass because they'd accepted other jobs. Since Glenis and I have known each other for a while, she asked me if I could recommend anyone as a replacement." Mandy raised her eyebrows. She bit her lip and grinned. "I immediately thought of you. I hope you don't mind, but I told Glenis about you."

"Me?" A prospect for teaching in London?

"Why do you look so shocked? That cookbook of yours is as good as any I've seen in a bookstore."

"Mandy, there's a big difference between writing a cookbook and teaching advanced bakers."

"In my opinion, writing a cookbook is a form of teaching. Plus, you said you've taught in your community and enjoyed it."

"I did, but the last class I taught was at the middle school."

"You underestimate yourself. Think of all the creativity and skill it has taken to create a month's worth of specials based on wartime recipes. You're a naturally engaging person with decades of experience." Mandy squeezed Janet's hands. "The London School of Cookery offers a prestigious program for advanced bakers. It could open a lot of doors for you." She loosened her hold and leaned against the gate. "You'd have to fill out an application, of course, and have an interview, that sort of thing, but you'd be a shoo-in. Especially with the benefit of a recommendation from another instructor."

"I'm not cool enough for a prestigious baking school." She tugged at the front of her SAVE THE WHEAT AND HELP THE FLEET T-shirt. "I wear tops with logos on them. I own like, one pair of dress slacks. And I've lost track of how long it's been since I changed my hairstyle."

"You would have a uniform."

Janet fought the urge to shudder. *A uniform?* She felt itchy and restricted just thinking about it. "I would look ridiculous in it."

"You would not." Mandy's face suddenly held the same expression as when she was twenty and trying to talk Janet into borrowing one of her trendy skirts. "No one at the school will care about your hair or what you wear in your spare time. They care about your baking ability, and yours is top-notch."

Janet pictured herself teaching alongside bakers with sophisticated British accents. "They'll make fun of my accent. I'll sound like a hick compared to everyone else."

"Then you'll be in good company. I have the same accent. For as long as I've known Glenis, she has never made me feel less than because of the way I talk. Though she has corrected my pronunciation of *scones* more than once. But that sort of thing can be learned."

"I suppose." *Scons.* The pronunciation had never made phonetic sense.

Another image took shape in Janet's mind of making a delicate layered trifle that might be considered a bit too extravagant for the Whistle Stop Café. The scene changed to her having high tea with Mandy at Harrods Department Store and a member of the Royal Family strolling by. "How long is the program?" She might be able to get away for a few weeks if she gave Debbie plenty of notice.

"Three months."

Janet's stomach sank. "That's right. You said it was for a semester." She couldn't be away from the cafe for three months. So much for high tea at Harrods.

"It starts the second week of September and ends in mid-December, in time for the holidays."

"That's a long time."

So why did everything about this opportunity sound like the best thing ever now that Mandy had assured her she wouldn't be laughed out of the place? Aside from anticipating a stiff uniform.

Teaching advanced culinary skills might be a nice challenge. She would get to travel, push herself as a baker, come home with new ideas for the café.

She counted the months in her head. Half of September, October, November, half of December.

She would be gone for Thanksgiving.

December was a busy time at the depot with the Christmas Train. Never mind her commitment to the café and time away from Ian.

"I don't think so, Mandy. Three months is too long for me to be gone. I appreciate you thinking of me." Why did she feel so disappointed? A trip to London hadn't been on her radar until Mandy came to town. She and Ian were planning a trip to Scotland.

"Aw, come on, Janet. Now that Tiffany's grown, this is your chance to get out of Dennison for a while, and earn money doing it. The school will even cover your travel costs. So, unlike in college when you didn't go to Italy because your parents couldn't afford it, money doesn't have to hold you back. It's a chance to get out of your same old rut."

Was she in a rut? "I don't feel like I'm in a rut."

"I didn't think I was in one either, until I took the chocolate making class in France and discovered how much I grew. Think of it as a step of faith."

A step of faith. Like when she accepted Debbie's offer to open the café together. It had been the best decision she'd made since saying yes to Ian's marriage proposal.

Was it time to step out in faith again?

It wasn't as if she planned to walk away from the café for good.

"I would have to think and pray about it. It's a lot to ask, especially of a business partner."

"Will you at least talk to your husband and Debbie?"

Janet watched a woman who looked about her age following her husband into the Pullman car. How long had it been since she and Ian went away for a weekend? If she did apply for the job and got accepted, maybe she and Ian could fly over the pond early and spend some time in England together before she started teaching. She'd have two trips to look forward to. "It would be pretty amazing."

Mandy put her arm around Janet and gripped her forearm. "Come on. I know you want to go."

London landmarks started flashing through Janet's mind like a slide show of someone else's vacation photos. Big Ben. Tower Bridge. The London Eye. Westminster Abbey. The more sucked in she got, the more she wanted to skip the parts that included praying and talking to those who would be most affected by her choice, and just say yes.

You co-own a café. Be realistic.

Janet shook herself back into real life with another reminder that Mandy's invitation wasn't a done deal. Even if Ian and Debbie gave her the green light, she still had to apply.

"I do want to go. But of all the qualified baking instructors your friend has to choose from, why would she pick a Midwesterner who spends her days flipping grilled cheese and keeping up with the cinnamon roll demand?"

"You'll never know if you don't apply."

Mandy's remark nagged at her as they walked back to the depot.

How would she know the answer to any of her questions—her qualifications, or if it was the right thing to do—if she didn't take the first step toward the possibility?

What if God had more in mind for her than working in bakeries and cafés in her hometown?

When would she get a chance like this again?

CHAPTER ELEVEN

Ian crossed his arms and leaned against the kitchen counter. "Three months?"

Janet had purposely waited until after Tiffany left to attend a meeting for the Memorial Day celebration to tell Ian about Mandy's invitation. Their transition from finishing up dishes to sitting down with cups of relaxing herbal tea felt like the best timing.

She took two matching mugs off the cute hanger Mom bought her for Christmas. "I know. It's totally impractical. The whole point of discussing travel the other night was for a trip of our own, not so I could traipse off by myself."

Ian took one of the mugs from Janet. "The only issue that makes it impractical is the café. You wouldn't be leaving small children behind."

"But the café is a big factor in all this."

Ian filled his mug with hot water. His pale blue eyes stayed stuck on the contents of his cup for so long that Janet wished she could jump inside his head to read his thoughts. Ian finally looked up. "An overseas teaching opportunity could be considered a sabbatical of sorts. Professionals take them all the time."

"I hadn't thought of that." It seemed a perfectly legitimate approach. Until she pictured Debbie running the café without her.

"A sabbatical that leaves my best friend in the lurch and you on your own."

"Leaving a co-owned business for three months is definitely a big thing to consider. But you have Paulette as an employee now. It wouldn't hurt to ask Debbie what she thinks about the idea of you applying." Ian took Janet's mug and filled it. "As far as me being on my own, I'm a big boy." He went to the cupboard and came back with their new favorite evening tea. "I certainly won't stand in your way if you want to apply."

"You wouldn't? Even if it means me being gone for Thanksgiving?"

"Someone in Dennison will take pity on me and Tiffany." Ian tore open two tea bags. He put one bag in his mug and the other in Janet's. "Or who knows, Thanksgiving in England might be fun for a change."

"They don't celebrate Thanksgiving in England."

"But they sell turkeys there. They have restaurants."

Janet reached for her mug. She bobbed her tea bag up and down. "You really wouldn't mind if I applied?"

"You said you wished you'd been brave when you had a chance. If you're accepted, this could be kind of like the semester abroad you never took. Plus, the money you earn teaching can help fund our family trip to Scotland."

"Oh, so that's why you want me to go."

Ian nudged her. He led the way to the living room. "Wouldn't it be fun to teach Brits how to bake like Midwesterners?"

"It would be fun." Assuming they didn't scoff. "I'm sure they'll be so impressed with my Americanized scones. Excuse me. *Scons*."

"You never know. They might discover that Midwesterners have a secret to the tastiest scones on the planet. Then you can introduce them to the wonders of dirt cake and buckeyes. Expand their horizons a little."

Janet set her mug on the coffee table and sank onto the sofa beside Ranger. "I didn't expect you to respond like this." She'd expected, "Wow, what an honor," followed by confirmation of her need to consider reality.

Ian sat beside her. "I say talk to Debbie. If she's on board, go ahead and apply and see what happens. You aren't committing."

"Okay, I'll talk to her about it tomorrow." Janet took a slow sip of her tea. It had a hint of lavender in it that calmed her senses like in an ad. "And to think that at noon today the biggest things on my mind were float sabotages and Harry's missing lantern. Speaking of which, wait till I tell you what Jim Watson brought into the café today."

A half hour before the café doors opened the next morning, Janet stood in the kitchen with Debbie.

"Are you kidding me? You're applying to go to England for three months?" Debbie's tone was playful, but when she didn't immediately express her feelings about the news, Janet took it as evidence that she didn't like the idea.

Janet took the bowl off the giant mixer against the wall. "Don't worry. I haven't applied yet. The time frame is a big deal, I know." Disappointment bubbled up. Getting the green light from Ian had felt like a sign that she should apply. Maybe she should've talked to Debbie before Ian got her hopes up.

Debbie scooted a set of measuring cups over to Janet. "It's a very big deal. What does Ian think?"

Janet scooped flour into the bowl for her morning batch of pancakes. "He supports the idea of me applying. He said I could think of it as a sabbatical. Not that we've been in business long enough to warrant one." They'd barely been open for two years. She scooped another half cup of flour.

Debbie leaned her hands on the worktable. She gave Janet a half smile. "Some professions require a certain number of continued education hours per year."

Janet added sugar. "But in this case, I'd be training other bakers."

"True. But what an experience." Debbie reached for the salt and handed it to Janet. "I wouldn't blame you at all if you want to do it. I'd certainly be tempted to apply. I mean, it's England. You would be an international baking instructor. What a fun piece of personal trivia to have handy for a getting-to-know-you mixer at church." She walked to the refrigerator and came back with a flat of eggs. "Think of all the new recipes you'd come home with."

"I thought about that yesterday. Teaching outside my hometown would force me to stretch myself."

"We could take this place up a notch." Debbie's face perked up. "We could start offering afternoon tea."

"Wouldn't that be fun?" Janet imagined herself serving Harry a tiered plate of delicate finger sandwiches and assorted sweets. It really didn't suit him. Patricia, on the other hand, would be all over the elaborate array. "I could relearn how to make croissants from scratch." Janet took a whisk off the hook on the side of the work area. "The process takes all day."

"We would even pronounce them correctly." Debbie attempted the French pronunciation and followed it up with a wrinkled face. "But yeah, three months is a long time for you to be gone."

"Plus the school only has one open slot. I doubt I would be the only one applying."

Janet cracked some eggs into another bowl, whipped them up, and transferred them to the mixer bowl. She added the rest of her ingredients in silence then turned the mixer on high, enjoying the hypnotic whir of the beater going around and around, while feeling Debbie's eyes bore into her in a way that made her feel slightly exposed. How could she leave her best friend? Spend three months in a place where she knew one other human, one she hadn't spent significant time with for years? She shut off the mixer.

"You want to apply, don't you?" Debbie's eyes stayed fixed on Janet.

I so want to. The idea of being in a strange country alone terrified her, but she still wanted it. "It's unrealistic." How many times would she say that? A stirring in her stomach told her being in a new place full of new people might also be kind of exciting. "I couldn't do that to you."

"It's okay to want to apply. I'll still be your best friend."

Janet turned to face the woman who knew her like family. Some things about her bond with Debbie went even deeper than family. "I do want to. But is it right for the co-owner of a café to run off to Europe for so long?"

"You would be guilty of running off if you said, 'Hey, Debbie, I sense God telling me that since I never backpacked through Europe in college, I should make it my midlife crisis activity.' Or 'Guess what, Ian surprised me with a cruise. It lasts three months. We leave next week.' But teaching. That's different. The semester starts in mid-September. It's May. I would have plenty of notice to find temporary help. And your reason for going would ultimately benefit the café."

Janet felt a lump rising in her throat even though she didn't feel sad.

"I'm not saying it would be easy running this place without you. But if God is opening a door, I'll support you completely. I wouldn't dream of holding you back from something like this." Debbie put her hand on Janet's arm. "You'd do the same for me."

Janet hadn't realized how badly she needed Debbie's blessing until she felt tears of joy prick her eyes. "Yes, I would do the same for you." She threw her arms around Debbie and gave her a tight squeeze. "That settles it. I'm going to apply."

Later, Janet poured three perfect circles of pancake batter onto the griddle. *I'm going to England.* Maybe. When the time came to flip them, she dared fling one high over the griddle, and it even turned midair and fell with a sizzle like a professionally flung pancake.

She delivered the plate to Debbie then took a picture of the specials board for posterity.

TODAY'S SPECIALS
BREAKFAST – SPAM & EGGS
LUNCH – CLASSIC EGG SALAD SANDWICH WITH CHOICE OF FRIES
OR SEASONAL FRUIT
SOUP OF THE DAY – TOMATO HAMBURGER
HOME FRONT BAKERY – HOMEMADE ENGLISH MUFFINS WITH
BUTTER & JANET'S STRAWBERRY JAM

Patricia ordered an English muffin, and Janet had to literally bite her tongue to keep from telling her about the baking school opportunity.

Harry arrived just in time to serve as a shift in focus.

"Good morning, ladies."

Patricia spread a big dallop of jam across her English muffin. "You're looking bright and chipper this morning, Pop Pop."

"What can I say? It's a beautiful sunny day. I'm about to eat a good breakfast and enjoy a rich cup of Debbie's coffee. And God sent a couple of nice volunteers to help me, Ray, and Eileen with our float."

Patricia slathered jam on her other muffin half. "I prayed that you'd find someone. Who's helping you?"

"Our two graduate students. When I went to Good Shepherd yesterday, Amber and Jasmine showed up, without their clipboards. They offered to help us with our float, saying they had plenty of vitals on each of us for now and wanted to know all about what we had in mind. We start building this afternoon. Turns out Amber's father is in construction, and she paid her way through undergrad by working for him during summer breaks."

Janet could see tall, curly-haired Amber in a construction hat. "Harry, that's wonderful."

"They also helped us come up with a solution for how to get the float finished without disrupting anything at Good Shepherd. We're going to work on it at my place."

Debbie set Patricia's peppermint mocha in front of her. "That's ideal."

Harry came over to the bakery case for a look. "A friend of Barry Smith is loaning us an old pickup truck to decorate and is driving it over today. The students talked to the director at Good Shepherd and got permission to use one of the vans to bring Ray and Eileen over to my house three days a week to get the job done."

Patricia got up to give Harry a hug. "This is better than you hoped."

Harry returned the hug then took a seat. "I do have one question for Janet and Debbie, though. Be honest with me now. Did you put a bug in Jasmine's and Amber's ears about offering to help and easing up on putting us under a microscope?"

They couldn't put anything over on Harry. "Guilty as charged," Janet said.

"But to be fair," Debbie added, "they asked for advice on how to better engage with you guys. They could tell you weren't having a good time. The part about asking for a van to drive everyone over to your place was all theirs."

"I hope we didn't overstep," Janet said.

"Not at all. I appreciate knowing they caught on that we were— how can I put it nicely?" Harry bugged out his eyes. "Bored stiff."

Patricia laughed so hard that she almost spilled her mocha. "Now you don't have to scale down your plan."

"Nope. In fact, it's going to be even better."

Janet was just opening her mouth to ask why when Charla Whipple blew in with a lively "Good morning!"

Charla's energy filled the café. Everything about Janet's former boss was bright—her smile, her personality, her red lipstick. She plunked a turquoise and white polka dot purse on the counter and gazed into the bakery case. "I need some sweet sustenance to get my day started."

Janet stepped up to the counter. Everything in her wanted to tell Charla about her baking school application. She would be thrilled. But if Janet applied and didn't get the job, she didn't want to have a long list of friends to tell the disappointing news. "Rumor has it you're in charge of the snack bar for the Memorial Day celebration," she said instead.

"That rumor is true." Janet noted an even brighter than usual shade of red on Charla's lips. "I'm also donating a dozen cupcakes for the cake walk. I couldn't say no to your daughter when she asked me."

"I couldn't say no to Tiffany either." She left out the part about cheating by offering extra of what she was already making. "What can we look forward to at the snack bar?"

"Hot dogs and corn dogs are a given. Cotton candy, of course. And we're renting an old-fashioned popcorn machine. I just got approval to buy the ingredients for something special—homemade Cracker Jacks complete with prizes. But I'm calling it Celebration Caramel Corn."

"Leave it to you to include prizes."

"It's not Cracker Jacks without a prize. I found some great stuff through an online catalogue. Plastic whistles, keychains, temporary tattoos, cute elastic rings, and tiny plastic bags to put them in."

Janet clapped her hands like an eager child about to see Santa. "Ooh, I want a tattoo in mine, please!"

Charla wagged her finger at Janet. "You get what you get, and don't have a fit."

Janet snapped her fingers. "Man." She grabbed her tongs. She snapped them open and closed, open and closed. "So, what baked treat can I get for you?"

"I think I'll have one of your homemade English muffins and jam."

Debbie reached for a small plate. "Good choice. I could gobble up Janet's strawberry jam by the spoonful."

Charla licked her lips. "When we worked together at the bakery, I often did eat it by the spoonful."

Debbie handed the plate to Janet. "So, Charla, I take it that with the snack bar, you're not also in on a float."

Charla shook her head. "From what I read in the paper, it's just as well. Let's hope this person doesn't decide to make the snack shack supply their next target."

Later, Janet repeated Charla's comment to Paulette while stirring up sourdough starter so it could rest overnight.

Paulette took a long whiff of the dough. "They better not mess with Charla's food. I haven't treated myself to caramel corn in over a year."

Debbie came through the double doors. She handed an order slip to Paulette. "Before you start that, I want to show you two something I found for the doughnuts we're passing out." She pulled up a stool. "Before I get too excited about them, Janet, do you have bags yet?"

"Nope." Janet tapped her wooden spoon on the side of the bowl to shake off remnants of dough.

"Good. If you had, I'd have to cry right here in the kitchen." Debbie held her phone out to Janet. "Look at these."

Janet set aside her bowl of sourdough and took Debbie's phone from her. As soon as she saw "Best Seller" at the top of the screen, she knew they had to have them. Each bag had a doughnut-related saying on it—SPRINKLED WITH LOVE, DOUGHNUT MIND IF I DO, THANKS A HOLE BUNCH.

"What do you think?"

Janet passed the phone to Paulette. "They're so cheesy. We must have them."

"Aren't they great?"

Paulette took her turn with the picture. "These are so hokey they're hilarious."

Debbie took her phone back. "I'm adding three packs to my cart right now. They'll take a few days." She gave the screen a stagy tap. "It'll be one less thing for me and Janet to look for at the party store this afternoon."

Janet tore off a sheet of plastic wrap and laid it over her dough. "My trunk is cleared out and ready to fill with all sorts of float decorations."

Debbie put her phone away. "I was so excited about the bags I forgot to mention that the order I gave Paulette is for Jasmine and Amber. They came in for lunch."

"Great, I can say hi before we get busy again."

Even over the Glen Miller album playing through the speakers, Janet could hear Jasmine and Amber laughing at their table in the far corner of the café. Two half-filled glasses sat between them.

Janet whispered to Debbie, "It's fun to see them acting like typical twentysomethings after all the seriousness last week."

"I think their subjects are rubbing off on them."

Janet could hear Paulette bopping along to "In the Mood" in the kitchen.

Debbie pointed to the bakery case with a menu. "Your English muffins were such a hit that the snickerdoodles got totally neglected."

Janet looked at the long row of cinnamon-sugar covered cookies. "Poor, sad snickerdoodles." The sound of Jasmine and Amber talking drew her eyes back to their table. "I'll see if they want some."

"Good idea. It beats them getting stale."

While pushing through the kitchen doors for a plate, Janet found Paulette doing a one-woman show in front of the fryer, swinging her hips and tapping the catchy rhythm with a spatula.

"You missed your calling as a drummer, Paulette."

Paulette whipped around, her cheeks a deep shade of pink. "What can I say? The tunes were a great choice."

Janet whisked up a plate. "Rock on, my friend."

Paulette pulled out the corners of her apron and curtsied.

Janet arranged four snickerdoodles on the plate and walked them over to Jasmine and Amber's table. "Do you girls want to rescue these cookies from feeling rejected because the English muffins were more popular? It would be a shame to have their self-esteem damaged." She placed the plate in the center of the table and took their empty dishes.

"Sure." Amber shut her laptop. "We can't have them feeling bad about themselves."

Jasmine took one. "They smell amazing. Thanks, Janet."

Janet smiled. "I appreciate your sacrifice. How about a refill on your drinks to go along with the cookies?"

"Yes, please. Mine is iced tea." Jasmine's phone buzzed. She moved her glass to the edge of the table then picked up her phone.

Amber handed over her glass. "I just had water."

"You got it."

Janet filled both glasses and added a little more ice to Jasmine's tea. When she returned to the table, the upbeat mood had been replaced by a gloomy cloud. Jasmine seemed to be fighting tears, her eyes glued to her phone screen. Amber shut her laptop.

Jasmine tossed her phone into her bag. "It's my own fault."

Amber reached across the table and placed her hand on Jasmine's arm.

Janet almost turned around to give them some privacy, until Jasmine straightened up and locked eyes with her. Jasmine swept her fingertips under her eyelids and pushed her long dark hair behind her shoulders.

Janet set Jasmine's tea in front of her. "Are you okay?"

"I'll be fine. Just, you know, life."

Janet gave Amber her water refill. She wanted to pull up a chair and let Jasmine pour out whatever had happened in the time it took to deliver refills. She looked so dejected. But she also knew enough about being young to understand that having a middle-aged woman intrude might not be welcome. "Listen, I need to get back to the kitchen, but if you need anything—"

"Thanks." Jasmine managed to smile.

"And I'll be here bright and early tomorrow if I can do anything to make, you know, life, any easier. As long as you're in Dennison, you're part of the community." Janet patted Jasmine's shoulder. "I'll leave you to your work."

On her way to the kitchen, she overheard Jasmine. "I shouldn't be shocked. Professor Chen warned me it might happen."

"Try not to panic." Amber's voice was gentle. "The decision isn't set in stone."

Janet resisted the urge to glance over her shoulder. *What just happened?*

CHAPTER TWELVE

Janet put her concern for Jasmine out of her mind to concentrate on float decorations. The party supply store was packed when she met Debbie there at three o'clock.

Janet pushed their cart around a graduation display to the aisle that sold art supplies. "Let's divide and conquer. I'll get markers and stencils for our sign, and you see if they have any patriotic streamers."

"Good call." Debbie took off toward the balloons and streamers aisle.

Janet zeroed in on a rack of crayons, colored pencils, and markers. Acrylic markers that claimed to write on any surface caught her eye. She took a twelve pack off the peg and started looking for large letter stencils.

She inched her way around a pair of young moms with toddlers. Their chatter carried across the aisle.

"Our dog was barking like crazy last night," one of the moms said. "John went outside but didn't see anyone."

"He shouldn't have gone outside." The other woman gave herself away as the bossy friend. "He should've called the police. It was probably that person who's tampering with the floats."

"We aren't doing a float."

"That doesn't mean they weren't in your yard after something else."

Janet tried to ignore the conversation behind her. The idea of someone sneaking around unseen felt too unsettling for a day of shopping for decorations. She found a disappointing selection of stencils.

Debbie came around the aisle waving two fat red, white, and blue spools. "I found the patriotic crepe paper," she sang. "I got the last ones." She dropped the spools into Janet's basket.

Janet flicked a package of number stencils. "The letters are picked over, unless we want itty-bitty ones. Maybe Tiffany has a set."

The two moms pushed their carts past Janet and Debbie, still exchanging guesses on who was in mom number one's backyard and why it probably had a connection to missing headlights and dumped potting mix. She watched them leave. "Now we need something for our sign."

"We might have to go to the fabric store for that. I read that vinyl works well." Debbie perused the selection of art supplies. "All we'll get here are premade signs."

A huge blue poster board with legs approached Janet. She edged the cart as close to the marker display as possible without causing a "Cleanup on aisle four" announcement. Debbie wedged herself between Janet and a sale display of sidewalk chalk. The walking poster board narrowly missed colliding with a rack of graduation banners.

"Excuse me," the pubescent male voice behind the poster board said. Tristan Eger's face appeared above it.

"Hi, Tristan," Debbie adjusted a stack of chalk tubs. "I don't think I've ever seen a poster board that large in person."

"It's for the float." Tristan tried to tuck the board under his arm and ended up whacking a woman behind him. He stepped aside. "Sorry."

The woman's expression reflected her feelings about kids shopping without parental supervision. "You should be more careful."

Tristan held the board over his head and let her pass. "I will."

Janet grabbed hold of one side of the board to help Tristan avoid another collision. "What's your theme?"

"My great-granddad was on a naval vessel during World War II, so I'm doing something around that. I'm starting with a sign while I figure out how to make something we won't have to buy look like a ship. Or at least the top of one." Tristan's poster board slipped from his fingers. He caught it before it hit the ground. "Mom and Dad are really stressed right now, so I told them I'd design the float. All they have to do is show up in the garage with power tools when the time comes to build."

"That's a big undertaking. I can't wait to see it."

Tristan backed up against a stack of party-favor-sized crayon boxes. Two boxes ended up on the floor. "I better go pay for this before I knock something else over."

Debbie reached down for the crayons and returned them to the shelf. "Good luck with your ship construction."

"Thanks." Tristan wove around a pair of teenage girls holding armfuls of prom theme decorations.

Janet choked back a chuckle. "I know I shouldn't laugh," she whispered, "but he looks so funny trying to manage that ginormous poster board." She pushed her cart past the girls. "I'm glad Kyle decided to enter the contest. It'll be good for the family to do something that gets their mind off roof repairs."

Debbie stopped beside a bin full of packs of balloons. "I'm trying to predict what he'll turn into a ship. I'm imagining an old wading pool with a poster board sail, but navy vessels don't have sails."

Janet considered the wading pool possibility. "It could end up kind of cute. Greg did say creativity in limited time is part of the fun."

Debbie tossed a pack of balloons into the cart. "I feel terrible even suggesting this, but—" She shot a quick glance in the direction Tristan had just headed. She lowered her voice. "Do you think it's possible that Tristan, you know?"

"No way." Janet saw Tristan at the register holding up his board for the cashier to scan. She waited for him to leave the store then confirmed that the pair of moms were long gone. "But now that you mention it, if anyone had a reason to want to win the competition, it's him."

After the shopping excursion, Janet dropped her bags on the big chair in the den. Then she headed to her bedroom and stared at the desk and her laptop sitting square in the center of it. She had one more thing on her agenda for the day. The application for the London School of Cookery.

"Hey, Tiffany," Janet called.

Tiffany came into the room with a big bag of plastic buckets in her hands. "Yeah?"

"How well do you know Tristan Eger?"

"Other than seeing him at the pool a lot when I lifeguarded last year, not very well. I know he's a good swimmer and always follows the aquatic center's rules. Why?"

Janet almost let Debbie's question about Tristan slip. "Just curious. Debbie and I saw him at the party supply store." She grasped for a legitimate change of subject. "Can you fend for yourself for dinner tonight? I need to get my application for the baking program in."

"Of course."

Janet sat at the desk. "So, what do you think about this whole idea of me applying to teach in London?"

"I think it's great. I'm proud of you."

"You are?"

"Are you kidding? Yes. After all the clubs and lessons and extra-curriculars you drove me to and paid for? It's about time you did something of your own."

Janet looked over at her beautiful daughter with her bag of buckets and realized she was experiencing what she'd heard older parents talk about—the stage when her child started to see her as a person. "That is so sweet of you."

"You can't stay in Dennison your whole life." The look in Tiffany's green eyes told Janet she might not become a woman who stayed in her hometown forever.

"I do worry that if you need me for something I won't be around."

"I can call Dad." Tiffany tucked her bag of buckets under her arm. She patted Janet's head. "I'll be okay. I know how to call 911, where the bandages are, and how to take my own temperature."

"You better get out of the room before your list of all the things you know how to handle without me drums up a barrage of worst-case scenarios."

Tiffany shut the door. She opened it a crack and poked her head back in. "Do you need a snack or anything? A cookie? Popcorn and diet cola?"

"I'm good. Thanks, sweetie."

"Okay. I'll be in my room decorating prize buckets if you need help. Feel free to put me down as a personal reference."

Janet laughed. "I wish I could." It had been years since she applied for a job. So long that when she opened the application link and saw a place to upload a résumé, she had to pause the process to update hers. She added her work experience at Third Street Bakery, the café, and the workshop she taught for the Culinary Arts Club at Dennison Middle School in September. She thought of her cookbook. Mandy would insist she include it, so she did. Before declaring the résumé finished, she decided to give it a fresh look with a new header and a picture that Debbie had taken of her at the bakery counter when they first opened. She flip-flopped between feeling unqualified calling herself a professional worthy of teaching more than local kids to recognizing how far she'd come since her days as a girl who would rather hang out in the kitchen baking brownies than do anything else. She had a flashback to a meeting with her high school guidance counselor during her senior year.

"What do you see yourself doing as a career, Janet?"

"*All I really want to do is cook and bake.*" She'd thrown out the idea of applying to culinary schools.

"*You can't make a career of baking cookies, Janet. Famous chefs are rare.*"

"*I don't want to be famous. I just want to pursue what I'm good at.*"

"*It helps to have a backup plan.*"

Yet, here she sat, listing all her experience as one who'd done exactly what her guidance counselor claimed she couldn't.

The evening light had turned a deep gold when she filled in the final question. She sat back in her chair and stretched her neck. She checked the time on her laptop. It was after seven.

A knock on her bedroom door startled her. Tiffany called from the other side, "I made dinner whenever you want it."

"You made dinner?"

"I found stuff for tacos."

Janet opened her bedroom door. "You are the best daughter ever. Give me five minutes."

"No rush."

Janet sat back down at her desk. She reread her responses, checked to make sure her résumé had uploaded, and corrected two wonky sentences.

She hovered her mouse over Submit. *Okay, God, here I go.* She clicked on the button.

Thank you for submitting your application.

There was no turning back now.

CHAPTER THIRTEEN

Sylvia checked the list her mother had given her for the market against the items in her basket. White bread, 1 pound bologna.... *She heard someone walking up behind her and moved aside to make way for them. Ray Zink inched his way around Sylvia.*

"Good morning, Sylvia." *He took a can of baked beans off the shelf and placed it in his basket.* "Looks like we both got grocery duty today."

Sylvia chose a can of the same beans Ray had taken. "My mother gave me a choice—going to the market for her or dusting the furniture."

"How's the Dennison Depot float coming along? I saw Bradley Macomb yesterday. He said he's helping you."

"He helped us come up with the design and is—" Sylvia caught herself before she let the lantern project out of the bag. Since suggesting they keep it a secret, Bradley hadn't even allowed Sylvia and Harry to see his progress. "Bradley's inviting some disabled veterans to ride on our float."

"One of my buddies lost his right leg on D-Day. He mentioned being asked. I haven't seen him so excited since high school when a pretty girl asked him to the Sadie Hawkins dance. And just so you know, making Bradley part of your committee has meant a lot to him. He's been making the best of his situation, but having something creative to do is bringing out the Bradley I went to school with before the war." Ray put another can into his basket. "We all need to feel like part of things, you know?"

Part of things was how Sylvia had felt while contributing to the war effort. Helping with the float was bringing that good feeling back. "Yes, I sure do."

By three o'clock that afternoon, Sylvia had eaten lunch, finished her chores, helped her mother decorate a sign for the bake sale, and headed over to the depot. By the time Harry announced that he'd finished for the day at five, Sylvia had sanded the window cut-outs on both sides of

their passenger car and set them against the maintenance shed for painting. She stood back from the shed
and admired her work. Now that the train had smooth
windows, she could see the design coming together.

Sylvia went into the shed for a can of gray paint
and brushes that Miss Eileen had bought. As soon
as Harry changed clothes and came out, they would
paint the first coat.

She heard something on the gravel behind her. She
set the paint can on the ground, stretched her back
and turned around. Margo stood there in her pristine
uniform and shoes as white as snow even after a full
Saturday at Fletcher Memorial Hospital. Meanwhile,
she looked like a girl who'd been working with wood
and sandpaper: sweaty, sawdust on her overalls, and
her hair poking out of its scarf. She wasn't put-
together, but at least she could greet Margo with a
smile. "Hi, Margo. Are you looking for Bradley?"

"Yes, I am. His parents invited me over for supper,
so I said I'd meet him here."

Harry emerged, dressed in old overalls and a paint-
stained work shirt. "Bradley's in the repair shed."

Sylvia brushed sawdust off her arms. "Otherwise
known as his studio."

"Thanks. It's fun to see him being secretive about
whatever he happens to be working on." Margo turned

in the direction of the shed then back around. "Your float is coming along beautifully. It's nice that you aren't afraid to get your hands dirty, Sylvia."

Sylvia felt blood rush to her cheeks at the thought of her appearance compared to Margo's. She tucked a stray lock of hair into her scarf.

Margo's eyes scanned Sylvia from head to foot. "I didn't mean... I meant it as a compliment. I know a lot of prissy girls who wouldn't come anywhere near sand-paper or a paintbrush."

Sylvia shoved aside the comparison game going on in her head. She didn't mind getting her hands dirty at all. In fact, she'd always found it quite invigorating and fun. She'd been one of those little girls who dug in the mud in the backyard with her brother while her friends played garden party. Funny, though, how the closer she got to adulthood, the more she cared about her appearance. "I'm my happiest when my hands are dirty. Are you helping with the hospital float?"

"No. The volunteers are in charge of that."

"You're welcome to help us. Miss Eileen encour-aged me and Harry to bring on as many volunteers as we need." Sylvia admired Margo's spotless shoes and delicate pink handbag. They could put her in charge of something ornamental. "We could use another girl. Someone with a knack for decorating."

"I'd like that. Thank you for inviting me."

"We're happy to have you."

Sylvia saw Miss Eileen walk in her direction then step away as if waiting her turn.

The corners of Margo's mouth turned up a little. "I do enjoy making paper flowers and stringing them for garlands. It'll give me more time out of the house and—" Her face tightened like she'd just caught herself saying the wrong thing. "What I mean is, helping with the float will allow me to spend more time at the station, now that Bradley is here so much." She gave a little wave. "I better go meet up with him. See you around."

Sylvia waved back. "See you."

Harry said goodbye and disappeared into the maintenance shed.

Miss Eileen shouted a quick good evening to Margo. She strolled over to the freshly sanded boards. "This is starting to look like a passenger car."

"Tomorrow after church, Harry and I are going to make a ramp for getting the two men in wheelchairs onto the float. And now we have Margo on the committee too, to help with decorations."

"I don't know how I would've gotten this done without you." She approached Sylvia. "I came over here because I remember you mentioning looking for a job for after graduation."

"Yes, ma'am, I am."

"Well, it just so happens that a friend of Rafe's is looking for a girl to answer phones and do some filing in his law office. I mentioned you to him. Before he posts the job, he'd like to know if you're interested in an interview."

Sylvia's heart leaped over the notion of having something to do after the float was complete and the parade a memory. She'd never dreamed of working in a law office. "Yes, ma'am. I need to ask my folks of course, but I'm sure they'll be happy about the idea."

Miss Eileen held out a business card. "Here's his name and number. I think you'll be a perfect fit. You're friendly, hardworking, good with people."

"Thank you, Miss Eileen."

"I hope it works out for you. It's not mechanic work, but maybe something different will be nice too."

Sylvia pictured Margo's squeaky-clean uniform and shoes. She saw herself sitting at a desk in a smart dress, answering the phone in a professional manner and directing the call to the appropriate line, filing folders in a tall cabinet. No women in her family had ever done such a thing. "I have a feeling it will be."

"All right then. Keep me posted on how things work out."

"I will. Thanks again." Sylvia found the cleanest pocket in the overalls for the business card.

Harry came out of the shed with a paint pan. "You ready to paint?"

Sylvia saw Margo and Bradley walking the path leading to the road. Bradley had hold of Margo's arm as they chatted away, oblivious to her and Harry. "They look so happy together."

Harry grabbed a paint stirrer and used it to pry the lid off the paint can. "Yep. Bradley is a lucky man. Almost as lucky as me."

Sylvia watched Harry as he dropped to both knees and started stirring the paint. She imagined him as her husband, getting ready to paint their house. Or maybe a baby's bedroom.

Harry looked up, his stir stick still dunked in the paint. "Hey, Sylvia."

"Yeah?"

"I love you."

Sylvia felt warm from head to toe. Warm and pretty. Harry had never said I love you *in words* before. Only in the way he treated her. She wanted to give him a big kiss like on VE Day. She opted for a more grown-up response. "I love you too, Harry."

CHAPTER FOURTEEN

*J*anet yawned. She'd been awake half the night overthinking her teaching application and hoping she and Debbie were wrong about Tristan. Especially after mentioning him to Ian.

The aroma of brewing coffee drew her from the kitchen to the café dining room. "Last night, Ian told me Tristan's name came up at the station as a possible suspect in the float vandalism. They don't have solid proof, only the common knowledge that he might feel desperate enough to win to sabotage others' efforts."

Debbie hit the button on the coffee maker. "I talked to Greg about Tristan too. Julian overheard us and said there's no way it's him. The night the Connor Construction float got messed with, Tristan had a soccer game."

"But do we know for sure he was at the game?"

"Julian remembers seeing a video on social media of Tristan making a great goal. His play won the game."

"I guess we're back to the drawing board." She held out her hand to Debbie. "May I have some of that coffee, so I don't fall asleep in the corn beef hash?"

Debbie filled a mug, poured in two vanilla creamers, and handed it to Janet. "We can't have that."

Janet took a long whiff and sipped with her eyes closed. "Aah. I'm glad it isn't Tristan."

"Me too. His family is going through enough."

When Janet opened her eyes, Mandy was opening the door to the café. "Good morning. I thought I'd see what today's Homefront Bakery special is before heading off to teach."

Kyle and Renee Eger walked in behind her and went straight to a table in the back without a word.

Janet took one more sip of her coffee before meeting Mandy at the counter. "We have molasses cookies today. They were extremely popular in the forties."

"I love molasses cookies. I have fond memories of dunking them in milk at my grandma's kitchen table. I'll take two and have them as a treat later."

Debbie said a quick hello to Mandy then picked up two menus and headed over to the Egers' table.

Janet dropped two fresh-from-the-oven molasses cookies into a bag. Her eyes wandered back to the Egers.

"So?" Mandy took a seat at the counter. "Did you apply?"

Janet set the bag in front of Mandy with a flourish. "I sent it last night."

"Yay!" Mandy pumped clenched fists. "Now my official recommendation letter will have an application to go with it."

"Was I supposed to get recommendation letters?"

"Technically, me telling Glenis about you counted as a recommendation letter. But I figured it wouldn't hurt to have it on paper as well. So I wrote one for you last night and emailed it to Glenis."

Debbie came up behind Mandy. "Is it too late to add another one?"

Janet stood with her hand on the counter, her lips frozen open in surprise.

Mandy rolled the top of the bag and slipped it into her tote. "I don't see why it would be."

"I want to write a recommendation for Janet."

Janet went over to shut the bakery case, finally finding her words. "You do?" She knew she had Debbie's support, but this took it to a new level.

"Of course. If you're going to do this, I want you to be fully equipped." She tore a page out of the middle of her order pad and slapped it down in front of Mandy. "Let me get your email address, and I'll send the letter this afternoon."

Mandy opened her purse and took out a pen. "See all the support you have in this. Now I'll have a friend to explore London with."

While Mandy jotted down her information, Janet forced herself to stop imagining the tea scene in Harrods again. "I haven't gotten in yet."

Mandy clicked her pen closed and handed the paper to Debbie. "You'll get in. You're a pro." She flung her tote over her shoulder. "I'm off to give a test on phyllo dough."

"Have fun."

Patricia passed Mandy on her way in.

Janet smiled at Debbie. Whether she ended up teaching in London or not, her dearest friend's blessing meant everything. It made her feel like the pro Mandy saw her as.

As Patricia sat down, Janet watched the Egers hunch over menus. They both looked so weary.

They ended up ordering coffees and muffins to-go and left without much more than hellos and goodbyes. If it wasn't Tristan damaging floats, could it be his parents?

Debbie sprayed whipped cream on Patricia's peppermint mocha. "I wish Greg could send a bunch of repair fairies to mend their roof."

Janet thought about thirteen-year-old Tristan with his poster board. Parents didn't always attend their kids' games.

Patricia stuck out her lip. "Stupid rainstorm."

Debbie leaned over to Janet and whispered in her ear. "Can I cheer us all up and tell Patricia where you might be going in the fall?"

Janet got a plate for the coffee cake Patricia had ordered. "Why not?" Now that she'd applied and Tiffany knew, it would be harder and harder for her to keep the prospect quiet.

Debbie delivered Patricia's drink. "Janet applied to teach at a baking school in London, England."

Janet saw a *What, you're moving?* expression on Patricia's face. Janet quickly specified, "For a semester. And it's not for sure. I only filled out the application last night."

Relief washed over Patricia's face. "Good for you."

"An old friend from college told me about it."

"Do you have a passport?"

"No. I guess I need to get one." Even if she didn't get the job, she would need it for Scotland. "I'll add that to my list of things to do."

"Selfishly, I will miss you like crazy. The café won't be the same without you. But I'll still be praying you get the job. How fun."

"I'm trying not to set myself up for disappointment by getting excited too soon."

Patricia reached for a fork. "Even if it doesn't work out for this year, the school will have your name for the future." She sank the fork into her coffee cake. "It could open up all kinds of things."

Janet saw an elderly couple from church coming into the café and prepared to excuse herself for fryer duty. "I hadn't considered that option." Judging from Mandy's enthusiasm, if Glenis decided against Janet, she could see Mandy begging Glenis to give Janet first consideration for next year.

Janet went to the kitchen to warm up the griddle.

Twenty minutes later, after serving up the corn beef hash the couple had asked to split, Janet went back out hoping to chat with Patricia. She'd already gone.

Debbie poured coffee into the couple's mugs. When she returned to the counter, the look on her face told Janet to prepare for upsetting news.

"The Great Float Bandit has struck again." Debbie nodded over her shoulder. "The Jacksons just told me."

The euphoria of surprise recommendation letters drained from Janet like air from a party balloon. "Who got hit this time?"

"One of the Girl Scout Troops." Debbie dropped the coffee carafe into its slot. "What does this person have against Troop 1096?"

"What does this person have against anyone?" Janet rubbed her temples. "Do you happen to know if Tristan's parents were at his game the night Greg's float got damaged?"

Debbie's face froze. "I'd never thought of them. I have no idea if they were there." She yanked her phone out of her pocket. "But if I can find Tristan's winning goal video, we might get a hint."

Janet reminded herself to breathe while Debbie opened the app, typed, and gave her screen a tap. She moved to Debbie's side and watched Tristan run up the field and evade the other players as Kyle Eger narrated the play. "And it's a goal!" The camera shifted to Renee in her screaming and jumping up and down soccer mom moment.

Janet let out her breath. "It wasn't them either."

The arrival of Pastor Nick and three men from the church cut Janet off from speculating with Debbie any longer. But alone in the kitchen, Janet tried to find similarities that connected the Dennison Police Department, Connor Construction, and Troop 1096 with Tristan Eger and his parents out of the picture.

When the breakfast rush wound down, Janet energized herself to spend the lull exchanging theories with Debbie while prepping Salisbury steak and the mashed potatoes she'd started before opening the café. Why these particular floats? She hadn't heard the extent of the damage to Troop 1096's float yet, but Ian's and Greg's had been minimal. So they weren't dealing with a hardcore vandal. She lifted the lid on her pot of mashed potatoes and gave them a good stir before heading out to explore her observations with Debbie.

Debbie pushed open the double doors. She had her phone in her hand and stress etched on her face. "Janet, I just got an alert for the pantry supplies order I put in the other day. It's running late. We won't get more flour, coffee, or cornmeal until Friday. Also, after what I just listed off, I feel like a pioneer."

Janet dropped her spoon into the heap of potatoes. "Your comment would be so much funnier if I wasn't doing extra baking for our specials this month."

"My sentiments exactly. I don't know what the hangup is."

Janet thought about what she had planned for the next day's menu. Now she knew what homemakers felt during wartime. "I'm fine on cornmeal. I can make the regular and gluten-free flour we have stretch for one day but not two." She put the lid back on her pot.

"A café cannot run out of coffee. I'll go to the big box store now while we're slow."

"I don't mind doing it. Getting out will keep me awake, and Paulette is due to arrive any minute. I'll buy enough flour and coffee to tide us over."

"I'll get the café credit card."

Janet set aside the potatoes. "I'll be back in half hour, tops."

Adrenaline drove Janet to shave the trip down to twenty-five minutes. She lugged two twenty-five-pound bags of flour into the depot by putting one under each arm and pushing the door handle with her fist.

Kim shouted to her from the museum ticket desk. "Do you need some help?" She dropped a stack of papers as she stood.

Janet set one bag on the ground to wipe her forehead with the back of her hand. "I'm ready for the wagon train."

Kim hurried over and held the door for her. "Want me to take one of those?"

Janet hoisted up the second bag. "I've got it for now." She stopped at the bench near the café for a rest. "Our delivery service let us down." She got ready to pick her load back up. "I better get inside with this. I still have coffee in the car."

"I need to get going too. A group of eighth graders is due in about thirty minutes. I called an extra volunteer to man the Victory exhibit." Kim picked up one of the sacks. "I need as many eyes on the museum as possible now that we've had a third incident."

Janet hugged the other flour bag to her chest, grateful to only be holding one. "You heard about that?"

Kim started toward the café. "When I called to confirm the arrival time for Mrs. Zane's social studies class this morning, she was rushing to the school after discovering that the tire pyramid in her Girl Scout troop's scrap and rubber drive float had been dismantled. Their signs and balls of newspaper were scattered all over her backyard. Thankfully, the tires aren't damaged, but she has a mess to clean up later and plans to report it to the police."

"When is this going to stop?" Janet took hold of the doorknob. The sound of another door slamming shut stopped her in her tracks. "Sounds like your volunteer just arrived."

"He arrived twenty minutes ago." Kim turned toward the noise. She dropped Janet's flour on the nearest bench. "It sounds like someone's in the storage room."

CHAPTER FIFTEEN

Janet left her bag of flour on the bench. She caught up with Kim in the hallway leading to the storage room where she kept old memorabilia no longer on display.

When Kim reached the door at the end of the hallway, it hung open a crack. Someone's navy and white tennis-shoed foot stood in the gap. Kim's volunteers always wore black shoes.

Janet heard items being moved around inside the closet. *Where's my rolling pin when we need it?*

Kim took a step closer to the door. She looked over her shoulder at Janet.

The door opened from the other side.

Kim and Janet jumped back and yelped in stereo.

Jasmine let out a screech. Harry stood behind her.

Kim's shoulders dropped with relief. "Harry."

Jasmine stood rigid then started laughing. "Sorry about that."

Janet put her hand over her racing heart. "What are you two doing here?"

Harry smiled as if nothing unusual had happened. He pushed the door closed. "The door slammed on us."

Kim shook her head and groaned. "When am I going to get that kick-down doorstop fixed?" She gave Janet an apologetic glance. "I gave Harry access to this closet for his float."

"We were looking for a substitute for something Harry hasn't been able to locate." Jasmine threw up her hands. "No luck."

Harry's demeanor changed from nonchalance to apologetic. "Kim, I should've checked with you before going in."

Jasmine cringed. "Sorry."

"It's okay," Kim said. "I'm the one who gave the go-ahead."

"We better go." Harry backed down the hallway. "Amber is Crosby-sitting."

Janet waved without saying anything.

"Jasmine," Harry murmured on his way out, "it's probably time to give up on this."

"Not yet. I think I know where we can find something similar."

Janet brushed flour off the front of her sweatshirt. "Ah, yes. Harry's secret float."

"In case you think I know what he's up to—I don't." Kim walked back to the waiting area. "I thought we'd caught our man. Or woman."

"So did I."

"If we could cross anyone off the list of suspects right off the bat, it's Harry Frankin."

"And Jasmine hasn't been in Dennison long enough to know who is entering the contest. Other than her focus group."

"And she seems too nice to have it in for anyone."

Janet considered what Kim had just said about Jasmine.

She waited until she'd gotten her flour and coffee into the kitchen before telling Debbie and Paulette what happened in the depot. She put on her apron as she spoke. "Whoever is tampering with the floats has to be a local, who knows who is entering the competition and where to find each construction area. Kim said something that made me rethink the possible motive." She opened the lid on the mashed potatoes. "Do you think it's some kind of revenge?"

Debbie took down a big salad bowl. "We do have two Girl Scout Troops in the competition."

"And," Paulette said as she tore open the bag of greens, "I happen to know they had a pretty intense rivalry during this year's cookie sale. It got downright petty if you ask me." She threw up her hands and almost dropped the salad bag. "They're cookies, girls. You weren't all up for the same full-ride scholarship to Harvard."

Janet dropped a pat of butter into the potatoes. "Their rivalry would explain Troop 1096's float. But not the others."

"Unless this person is mad at the whole town," Debbie suggested.

Janet paid attention to her potatoes. Who would be mad at the whole town?

Tiffany sat on the foot of Janet's bed holding a three-pack of toy fishing poles. "They took apart a Girl Scout troop's tire pyramid? That's just mean." She pulled the cardboard backing off her package of poles.

Janet did a mental inventory of documents she needed for her passport application according to the US State Department website. She adjusted the pillows behind her back and wrote the list on a notepad beside her on the bed. "So far, the only answer we can come up with is that this person has a chip on their shoulder and is doing it out of anger."

Laddie woke up from a nap beside Tiffany. He sat up and stretched his front legs.

Tiffany stroked his back. "Who would have a vendetta against the police department, a construction company, and the Girl Scouts?"

Janet opened the online passport application. "Who knows. Like I told Debbie and Paulette, it has to be a local."

Tiffany tucked the cardboard under her arm. "Well, I better let you finish your application. I'm meeting Layla and Catherine to pick out costumes."

"Your dad is taking me to get my passport photo taken as soon as he gets home. Then I want to be the first to see your costume."

Tiffany shook her head. "Nope. You have wait for parade day like everyone else." She did a hair flip. "Haha." She marched out.

Janet shouted after her, "What if I decide not to make your doughnuts, young lady?"

"It'll be totally worth it."

Janet chuckled. She wouldn't dream of not making the doughnuts, but it was fun to pretend. She entered her first, middle, and last name into the application. Her mind drifted to thoughts of dismantled tire pyramids and melting light bulbs.

Laddie yawned and moved to the spot beside Janet. He stared up at her.

"What do you think of all this, Laddie? Do you have any suspects? I am at a total loss."

The next day Janet was cleaning the griddle in preparation for lunch when Debbie poked her head between the kitchen doors. "Janet, we have a party out in the dining room who'd like to say hello."

Janet tossed aside her sponge. "Be right there. Let me wash my hands."

Out in the dining room, she saw Jasmine pushing Ray Zink's wheelchair up to the head of a row of pushed-together tables in the center of the café. Amber held a chair for Eileen at the other end of the table while Harry looped Crosby's leash around a chair. The whole group wore work clothes, but the mood in the room felt like a party was about to start.

"What a nice surprise."

Debbie picked up a stack of menus and started handing them out.

Jasmine took a seat between Harry and Eileen and put one arm around each. "We thought it would be fun to have an early lunch before working on the float at Harry's."

"It's painting day," Eileen said.

Ray looked over his menu at Eileen. "The last stage before we put on the final touches."

"For now," Harry added, "it's locked up tight in my garage."

"What's your wartime lunch for today?" Eileen craned her neck and looked over at the specials board. Her eager expression melted into as close to disgust as a good-hearted woman like Eileen could manage. "Am I really reading jellied chicken, or are my eyes failing?"

Ray shook with silent laughter. His gaze settled on Eileen like he thought she was the funniest person on the planet.

"You aren't seeing things," Janet told her. "Gelatin helped families stretch all kinds of things."

"Oh, I know. It was all the rage." Eileen went back to reading the regular menu. "I just don't know who thought it would be a good idea to combine gelatin with something other than fruit."

Ray peeked over his menu at Eileen, his eyes alight like a middle schooler with a crush.

Okay, Ray Zink. Janet watched him watch Eileen while Debbie took drink orders. *This admiration from afar has gone on long enough.*

She waited for what felt like the right time to approach Ray. It came after the group had eaten, visited, and were on the way back to the van.

Amber took hold of the handles of Ray's wheelchair and pulled it away from the table.

Janet cut in. "I'll take Ray. We haven't chatted in a while."

"Okay. See you at the van, Ray." Amber held her arm out to Eileen instead. They walked ahead. Out in the waiting area, Amber said something to Eileen that made her laugh.

Ray started chucking again. "Doesn't Eileen have a beautiful laugh? It always makes me want to join in."

"She sure does." How many other hundred-plus-year-olds still had their sense of humor intact? Janet parked Ray's chair right outside the café.

"And she has such beautiful blue eyes."

For years, Janet had recognized the soft spot that Ray had for Eileen Palmer. But today felt different. He was downright smitten with her.

Janet knelt beside Ray's wheelchair. "Eileen looks pretty today. Even in old jeans and a T-shirt." In all the decades that Janet had known Eileen, the woman had never lost her sparkle.

"She looks twenty years old again."

At that moment, Ray seemed younger too, even sitting in a wheelchair in a faded work shirt for painting day.

"You know what, Ray?"

"What?"

"I think you should ask her out."

Ray whipped his head around so quickly that Janet almost forgot he was in his late nineties. "Oh, you're kidding around."

"No I'm not. I think you should ask Eileen Palmer out on a date."

Ray waved his hand in Janet's direction. Within seconds, he went back to watching Eileen. "People our age don't go on dates."

"Since when? There's no age limit on dates that I know of."

The corners of Ray's mouth turned up. "Come to think of it, I haven't heard of one either." He leaned his head toward Janet's. "Where could I invite her to go? I can't drive her anywhere."

"How about one of the activities at Good Shepherd?"

"Now there's a thought. We have movie nights every week."
Janet pulled herself to a standing position. "There you go."

"You don't think it would be, as you kids say, too weird?"

"Not at all."

CHAPTER SIXTEEN

Sylvia ran her hands along the smooth surface of the wooden passenger car. She'd hurried from school to home to drop off her books and change clothes, then to the depot to talk to Miss Eileen and finish the float with Harry. The parade was on Saturday. They needed to get moving.

"Harry, it's all done." Someone had attached every piece of siding, fitted the shell to the bed of Mr. Palmer's old Ford, and stenciled DENNISON DEPOT *along each side. Just as she'd hoped, the makeshift passenger car fit perfectly over the bed, thanks to beams nailed to the inside.*

"Surprise!"

Sylvia peeked into the back of the truck. It had a simple bench seat over the tire humps and handles below each window. The ramp that she and Harry had built after church the day before lay against the left bench. "Who did all this?"

"Me, Mitch, Rafe Palmer, and Miss Eileen." Harry came to Sylvia's side behind the truck. He pulled on the latch that lowered the platform. "Miss Eileen felt bad for not being able to help more, and Mr. Rafe wanted to contribute somehow, so they built the benches on the sly. We put it all together after you went home yesterday. Miss Eileen did the stenciling." Harry grabbed her hand. "Come look what else Mr. Rafe did."

Sylvia managed to keep up with Harry while still admiring the windows and perfectly straight lines painted over and beneath the station name. "Who did the windowsills and details?"

"Me."

"You did a fine job."

"I figured you did the sanding, so it was my turn." Harry backed up and pointed to the front of the shell. "Mr. Rafe rounded the corners to match the curve of the cab, to make the shell look more like part of a train. He did the same thing in back."

"It's even better than I hoped."

"Now all we need is Bradley's lantern and your sign."

She'd been so busy with building the float that all she'd done for the sign was cut a big piece of cardboard from an old refrigerator box a man at the appliance store let her have. "I can work on that today now that the float's done."

"I can help you since it's my day off." Harry went outside the maintenance shed and looked around. "I haven't seen Bradley since I got here to meet you. He's usually here almost every day."

Sylvia gave the float a final once-over. "Maybe he needed a day off to let his idea simmer. He told me the other day that he always does that when he's sculpting." She backed her way to the door to see what the passenger car looked like from a different angle. She imagined it in a line of other floats, led by Miss Eileen holding a ribbon-streamed lantern she was still waiting to finally see.

Outside, she reached into her pocket and took out a folded half sheet of notebook paper. "Look what I have." She held the paper in front of Harry. "An official interview appointment, tomorrow at four o'clock."

Harry wrapped his arm around her and drew her close. "Congratulations."

She was opening her mouth to thank Harry when she spotted Margo and Bradley on the sidewalk leading to the station. Margo had Bradley on one arm and a handled shopping bag on the other. The two looked different than on Saturday when they walked off smiling to have dinner with Bradley's parents. They both seemed to have heavy feet and giant weights on their shoulders.

Margo pointed to Sylvia and Harry and said something to Bradley.

Sylvia waved to them. Harry shouted hello. By the time Margo and Bradley stood in front of Sylvia, their mouths smiled but their eyes didn't.

Margo held out the shopping bag. It had Sylvia's name written at the top in neat script. "I made a bunch of flowers for the float after church yesterday."

Sylvia took the bag and thanked her. She pulled apart the handles. The bag was filled to the brim with delicate tissue mums, poppies, and roses. "You made all this in one afternoon?"

Margo nodded. "I'll make more tonight."

Bradley moved the tip of his cane in little circles on the ground as if drawing a picture only he could see. "I'll be back tomorrow to finish my part of the float."

Sylvia turned and pointed with the bag toward the maintenance shed. "The float's finished. Do you want to see it?"

"Maybe tomorrow." Bradley took hold of Margo's arm again.

Margo said a quiet, "Bye."

They walked away, leaving Sylvia holding the bag of lovely paper flowers. "What happened?" she wondered to Harry.

The following afternoon, Sylvia strutted out of Peterson's Law Office feeling three inches taller and all grown up. She hugged a training booklet against her chest. She wanted to tell everyone she passed about her job. Her father had been so proud of her when she told him about the opportunity that he'd offered to pay for a new work dress and shoes if she got the position.

"It's not every day that a young woman gets an invitation to interview for an office job."

He'd called her a young woman. Not a young girl.

She passed the park across from Fletcher Memorial Hospital. Margo stood beside one of the big oak trees in her uniform. Sylvia ran toward the park, stopping only to check for cars at the edge of the sidewalk.

"Margo!" Sylvia waved.

Margo barely looked up. She shifted around to one side and brushed her hands across her eyes. She turned around and gave a half wave.

When Sylvia reached Margo, she took a moment for a quick breath. "I showed Miss Eileen your flowers. She said they're the best paper flowers she has ever seen."

"That's kind of her." Margo's eyes were red and puffy. "You look extra nice today. And excited."

"I just had an interview and got a job answering phones and taking appointments at a law firm," Sylvia responded, beaming with pride at her accomplishment.

"Good for you, Sylvia." Margo's voice sounded tight. She glanced Sylvia's way only to avert her eyes again. She gazed at her white shoes.

"Hey. Are you okay?"

Margo sniffed and nodded. But Sylvia could see her bottom lip trembling.

"You don't look okay."

Margo's face scrunched up. Tears trickled down her cheeks.

"What happened? You can talk to me." Sylvia glanced over the shoulder to check for other people. *"Did you and Bradley have an argument?"*

Margo uncrumpled a handkerchief in her hand and wiped her eyes. "No, it's nothing like that. It's my parents." She wiped her cheeks with the white hankie and took a shaky breath. *"They want me to break things off with Bradley."*

"Why?"

Margo leaned against the tree trunk. "Why do you think? Because he's blind." She let her arm drop and gave her leg a little punch. *"They won't stop talking about it. My dad even brought it up with Bradley yesterday. It humiliated him."*

"But you clearly love Bradley. And he adores you. What more could your parents want?"

Margo stared off into the distance. "They don't want me to marry a man who can't work." She faced Sylvia. A mix of anger and grief filled her hazel eyes. *"This morning at breakfast Dad said, 'We didn't put you through nursing assistant school so you could become the breadwinner.' Then Mom joined in, 'What if there's an emergency? Bradley can't drive a car.'"*

"But you can drive." Sylvia had seen Margo driving when it was too cold to walk to work.

"That's what I said." She brushed away another tear. "Mother asked what I'll do once we have children. I told her Bradley would be a wonderful father. I've seen him with his younger cousins. But Mother said Bradley would be one more child for me to care for. I told her she was being cruel to compare Bradley to a child. Dad ordered me to apologize as if I was a little girl myself." Her voice broke. "It was horrible."

Sylvia turned her head toward the road leading to the train station. She'd seen Bradley go into the repair shed and hang the ARTIST AT WORK sign when she stopped by to store her parade sign inside the float. He'd designed their float in his head. "He seems perfectly capable of working to me. I wouldn't be able to manage what he's doing even with vision, and mine is twenty-twenty."

"But he doesn't have a steady job." Margo scowled in a way that Sylvia hadn't realized she had in her. She was always so gentle and soft-spoken. "It's as if my parents assume Bradley and I haven't considered all the things they brought up. Bradley doesn't want me to be the breadwinner either. I haven't told anyone this, but he tried to break things off when he came home from the convalescent hospital. He told me he wanted me to be free to have a happy life."

"Since you're still together, I take it you told him you would be happiest with him."

"Yes. I reminded him that if he'd been blinded when we were already married, no one would expect us to separate. So why separate for such a thing now? When people genuinely love each other, they stick together. They help each other through tough times."

Sylvia tucked the training booklet under her arm and nervously bent the cover of it. The whole conversation felt different from what she was used to with school friends, even when they had boy trouble. It felt so much more serious. What could she say to make Margo feel better? She watched Margo tuck her hankie into her purse and take out a compact and a tube of lipstick. Margo was nineteen. The same age Mama was when she married Dad. *Aunt Marion had married at eighteen.*

"I can't tell you what to do. But the way I see it, you're a grown woman. And Bradley is a man who has already fought in a war." She thought of a school friend whose older sister waited for her boyfriend to come home from the war. They weren't together anymore. *"I know of some men who came back from the war so scarred—physically, or in their mind—that their girlfriends couldn't handle it."*

"That's what I told my mother before leaving for work today. Bradley could be extremely bitter right now, but he isn't. He wants to work. He helps his mother with housework sometimes just to keep busy." She opened the compact and checked her face. She groaned. "I look a mess."

Sylvia stroked Margo's arm. "Splash a little water on your face in the ladies' room. That'll help."

Margo snapped the compact shut. "Bradley found out about a school for the blind that works with veterans. It's in New York. He talked to the VA about registering. He is so determined. But all my parents see is his blindness. Dad said he won't pay for me to continue my nursing training to become an RN if I stay with Bradley." Her eyes filled with tears again. "What am I going to do, Sylvia?"

Sylvia held her folder with both hands and tapped it against her leg. What would she do if Harry got permanently injured while working at the station?

She didn't even have to think about it.

"Since you're asking, I think you should stand by the man you love."

CHAPTER SEVENTEEN

Patricia was moving off her stool to the register when Janet came out of the kitchen with a fresh-from-the-oven plum charlotte for Monday's Homefront Bakery special.

"That sure is a pretty cake."

Janet held up the plum charlotte. "The ingredients are simple, but it sure was fun to make." She set it on the counter. "Guess what I did last night? I got my very first passport picture taken. I was so tired that the picture turned out as terrible as everyone talks about. I felt like I'd joined the in group."

Patricia held out her fist. "You go, girl!"

Janet fist-bumped Patricia. "But it did feel strange to be told I couldn't smile. A passport is a ticket to adventure, and we don't get to smile?"

Debbie stuck Patricia's card into the reader. "Maybe they want to make sure you look like the version of yourself *after* you've gone through airport security, customs, an eight-hour flight, and jet lag."

"That must be it." Janet found a place for her plum charlotte, right up front in the case.

Patricia put away her credit card. She set a cash tip in front of Debbie. "They should take two pictures. A serious one and a 'Yay, I'm in Europe!' one."

"I agree."

Patricia made her way to the door. "I caught a peek of Faith Community Church's float last night. They're doing a Pray for the Troops theme. It's beautiful."

Debbie put the tip in her pocket. "They better wrap it in barbed wire. The parade is six days away, and the culprit is still out there."

Janet spent the first part of the morning flipping pancakes, frying scrambles, and fighting a strange ache in her heart. If she got accepted for the teaching position, she would miss out on things like daily visits from Patricia for her peppermint mocha and sweet treat.

She'd secretly wondered on many occasions why Patricia never got tired of having the same coffee drink day after day or never went on a health kick. In all her professionalism and ability to help Janet and Debbie when they needed legal advice, Patricia remained the same fun-loving regular with her sweet tooth and love for her grandfather.

I'm going to miss Harry.

And Crosby.

Janet shook herself back into the reality that she didn't officially have the position yet. She checked her watch. Ten thirty. She'd planned to leave early to get ready for Debbie and Paulette to come over for a sign-making party.

Debbie reached through the double doors with an order slip. "One grilled cheese on sourdough. It's a to-go order for one of the Pullman cars."

Janet took the slip from Debbie. *Do they have grilled cheese in England?* She couldn't imagine going three months without one.

The double doors flew open again. "I'm here." Paulette hung her purse on a hook. She took the slip out of Janet's hand. "I'll take care of the grilled cheese. In England they call grilled cheese sandwiches toasties. Isn't that cute?"

"It is." Why did having Paulette take over so quickly and eagerly make her kind of sad? It was time for her to leave anyway.

Out at the counter, Janet couldn't bring herself to rush off.

Debbie put her hands on Janet's arms from behind and scooted past her. "You can go. I know you have stuff to do before tonight."

Ellie Cartwright came in looking nothing like the friendly Claymont Library head that the people of Uhrichsville and Dennison knew her as. She slogged over to the counter. She hung one of two big bags with the swirly CRAFTY'S ART SUPPLIES logo over her arm. "Debbie, do you mind if I work at one of your back tables for a while? Don't worry, I'll order something."

Debbie handed her a menu. "Not at all. We're slow right now. What can I get for you?"

Ellie blew through pursed lips and read the specials board. She checked the bakery case. "What's plum charlotte?"

"It was a way to use up stale bread and fruit," Janet told her. "Since plums aren't in season yet, I used plum jam, and day-old pound cake instead of bread." The more vintage recipes she had to come up with for specials, the more she enjoyed the challenge of changing them up.

"Sounds good. I'll have a piece of plum charlotte, a large latte, and a giant pillow to punch, please."

Janet savored the moment of talking to a local who didn't come in daily. "Uh-oh. Bad morning?"

"You could say that. This is usually my day off. I planned to work on a dried flower wreath I'm making for the library's float. Instead, I spent two hours scouring the county for red poppy garlands like ones I hung the other night. I ordered them online, and I don't have time to wait for delivery again."

Janet squeezed her eyes shut. "I don't even have to ask what happened." She added the library to her mental list of seemingly random entries that she knew must have a connection. "So now we've had four floats tampered with and a close call with the fire department."

Ellie dropped her bags on the floor. "This whole thing makes me mad. The library is honoring Dennison service personnel who lost their lives in World War II. I still have a lot of work to do on the wreath. One of our regular volunteers for children's story hour is a lettering artist and is working hard on a sign. None of us has time for this sort of thing. Well, one of my volunteers does, but she's offended that I didn't ask her to do the lettering, so she's being pouty right now."

Debbie returned Ellie's menu to the stack. "I'm so sorry."

Janet got a plate for the plum charlotte. "Just out of curiosity, where do you keep your float when you aren't working on it?"

"In the employee parking lot behind the library. I'm sure some will say I should've known better after what happened to the others, but where else am I supposed to keep it? We covered it with old bed sheets." Ellie unzipped her purse. "Stupid me."

"No." Not unless the Dennison Police Department was also stupid. "You should be able to leave a project out and feel confident that it will still be there in the morning."

"I chose red poppies because they honor sacrifice and are meaningful at Memorial Day. They were hard to find, so close to the holiday. Now every website has them listed as either out of stock or with a June delivery date." Ellie lifted both bags. "I found one craft store thirty minutes away with all the supplies for making some garlands myself, so that's what I'm doing. We'll have about half of what we put up, but at least we'll still have red poppies." She let her bags drop to the floor again. "It's not the end of the world, but what a pain."

Janet looked at the clock, then at Ellie. She considered how far away she would be from familiar faces if she ended up in England for three months. "Do you want some help?"

"Would you?"

"Of course. I'm not as artistic as you and your story lady are, but I know how to use scissors and string and follow directions."

"I will love you forever."

Janet slid open the bakery case. "Debbie, make that two lattes. And I'm taking two servings of plum charlotte from the case."

"Janet's is on me." Ellie reached into her overstuffed purse. "It's the least I can do."

Janet scraped a spatula under the biggest, most perfect square of plum charlotte for Ellie then plated another for herself. She got two forks and walked them to an empty table for four to provide space to work.

Ellie came over and dropped her bag on the chair closest to the wall. "That dessert smells divine."

"It tastes pretty divine too, if I do say so myself. I sampled it this morning. I figured I couldn't serve it to customers without a test. Some of those rationing era recipes can be hit-or-miss."

"Have you had a miss yet?"

"Yes. Yesterday. We offered jellied chicken. People grew extremely fond of gelatin during the war, so I thought I'd try a savory version. Debbie and I thought it was tasty. Customers took one look at the name and practically gagged."

Ellie stuck out her tongue. "It resurrects memories of trying to choke down shrimp aspic salad at my grandmother's house every Easter. Sorry. Not a fan."

"I don't blame you. Even Eileen Palmer made a face. All but one serving ended up in the trash."

Debbie came over with two steaming lattes. "I overheard you talking about the jellied chicken episode." She set one latte in front of Ellie and the other in front of Janet.

Ellie added a packet of sugar to her latte and took a sip. She stuck her fork into her plum charlotte, raised it to her mouth, and chewed slowly. She closed her eyes. "Mm. The future is looking brighter now."

Janet stirred her latte and reveled in the joy of Ellie being refreshed by something she'd baked. If she got the job in London, maybe that could be part of her teaching—encouraging her students to love others through their baking.

The entrance door opened with a cheery ding. In walked Harry and Crosby with Jasmine. Janet waved to them. "Hey there, friends."

Crosby led the way to Janet and Ellie's table.

"Hold on, boy," Harry waited for Crosby to heel. "I know you're anxious to see Janet, but you still need to follow the rules."

Crosby slowed his pace. He stopped beside Janet and sat on his haunches.

Jasmine patted Crosby's back. "Goofy boy."

"You're a good dog, Crosby." Janet rubbed his head. "I know. I could hardly wait to see you too. It has been a whole day."

Harry said hello to Ellie and introduced Jasmine to her.

Janet detected a relaxed sense of joy in Jasmine. Whatever "life" thing had upset her the week before clearly hadn't done permanent damage to her psyche. She seemed as at ease with Harry as with Amber. "Are you two here for lunch, or for treats?"

"Treats." Jasmine wandered over to the bakery selection.

Harry stayed by the table. "We finished painting yesterday, so Jasmine suggested celebrating with cookies before moving on to decorations."

"Um, correction. You pushed for the cookies."

Harry cocked his head toward Jasmine. "She wanted to do something healthy like fruit salad because we're having a pizza party when the whole job is done." He called over his shoulder to Jasmine. "Pick out something that's bad for me."

Debbie went to the bakery area.

Ellie moved her plate aside and took one of the bags from the chair beside her. "I suggest you keep an even closer eye on your float, Harry."

Debbie called from the counter, "See, I told you barbed wire would come in handy."

"Barbed wire?" Jasmine let out a laugh. "Do you even have that here?"

Janet poked at her plum charlotte, determined to make it last. "Ellie's float was the latest casualty."

Jasmine cringed. "Again?"

Harry's whole body drooped with sympathy. "I'm sorry to hear that, Ellie. Fortunately, we don't have anything especially valuable on our float."

Jasmine shot a glance at Harry. Before Janet could read her expression, Jasmine turned back around and ordered three peanut butter cookies and three chocolate chip.

Debbie started bagging up the cookies. "Monetary value doesn't seem to matter."

Ellie emptied bundles of artificial poppies on the table. "They stole poppy garlands from the library float."

Janet took a bundle of poppies and tore off the paper wrapping. Debbie was right about the monetary value. Nothing this person took added up to much financially.

Debbie handed Jasmine her cookies. "So far this person has taken Ellie's garlands and Ian's light bulbs, has dismantled a tire pyramid, and made a mess of a victory garden."

"What is this person trying to do? Collect props for their own float?" Harry met Jasmine at the register.

He set cash on the counter. Jasmine gave it back to him and offered her card to Debbie. Harry made a second attempt to pay by laying his cash over the card. Jasmine took the bills, put them into Harry's palm, closed his fingers around it, and patted his hand. At the same time, she slyly tapped the card reader with her other hand.

"Haha. I won."

"All right," Harry said with warmth in his voice. "But I'm getting the next order."

Janet tried to watch them without openly staring. There was a friend-that-feels-like-family tenderness about them.

Ellie separated a bundle of flowers and spread them in the center of the table. "Wouldn't that be interesting if Harry was right?" She reached for her latte and took a sip.

Janet opened another bundle. "Do you think someone would have the nerve to show up to the parade with a float full of stolen props?"

"Stranger things have happened."

CHAPTER EIGHTEEN

Harry whistled a tune on his way out of the depot after a short after-school shift. He watched an eastbound train pull out of the station. Soon, if things worked out as Miss Eileen suggested, he would be spending days at a time on one of those trains.

A louder whistle overpowered his. It was a sort of whistle for getting someone's attention. Harry looked around and saw Bradley at the foot of the platform steps.

"Harry." Bradley's demeanor was a blend of excitement, nervousness, and satisfaction. "I have something to show you."

"How did you know it was me?"

"I'd recognize that whistle anywhere." Bradley waved Harry over. "Come with me."

Harry ran to follow Bradley. Something seemed different about him. What's changed? Other than him not seeming as distant as when he and Margo dropped off the paper flowers? Harry observed him as they walked. Bradley had a bounce in his step. He held his cane, but it barely hit the ground. He led the way to the repair shed with confidence and navigated the little room like one would his own home.

Bradley turned his back to the worktable. "I'm about finished with the lantern and need someone with decent eyesight to give it a once-over."

Harry closed the shed door. "I can't wait to see it."

Bradley's expression made a sudden shift from confident craftsman to insecure boy. He paused and took a long breath. "Close your eyes."

"Okay. They're closed."

He heard a clank of steel against wood.

"Before you open them, keep in mind it's not quite done. I still have some finishing touches to add. Sylvia is going to add ribbons and flowers, so that'll help too."

"You aren't being graded, Bradley. This is for fun."

"I know, but it's for the community. I want it to be good."

"I promise not to play art critic." As if he'd even know how to critique such a thing.

"Okay. You can open your eyes now."

Harry's lids opened to the sight of a lantern so unique that Harry only knew its previous state because he'd been the one to find it in the scrap box. It looked better than brand-new.

"I hope it's as nice in real life as in my head."

"Bradley. That is beautiful."

"Beautiful as in truly good, or good for a guy who can't see?"

"Beautiful as in, I've never seen anything like it. What needs improving?"

The entire surface of the lantern was clean and polished. Bars that were bent when Harry found the lantern now looked perfectly angled. Alternate sections of glass surrounding the lamp had been removed and replaced with thin plates of ornately designed steel with patterns of stars carved into them.

Bradley set the lantern on the worktable. "The handle and some of the bars were rusty, so I replaced them with some from an old camping lantern I found in our garage at home."

"I don't know what else to say. I'm just amazed by what you made."

Harry heard Sylvia calling his name from outside.

Bradley shook his head. "I don't want anyone else to see it until I'm finished."

Harry opened the shed door, just a crack. "Wait for me by the float. I'll be right there to help you decorate."

Bradley draped a heavy cloth over the lantern. "Before you go, will you make me a promise?"

"Sure."

"When it's finished and ready for the parade, I don't want anyone except you, Sylvia, and Miss Eileen to know I made the lantern."

"Why? People will ask when they see it in the parade. They might even want one just like it."

"Tell them it was a gift to the town of Dennison from a local artisan who wishes to remain anonymous."

"I don't understand. Why wouldn't you want people to know what you're capable of?"

"It's hard to explain." Bradley shifted his weight so his back rested against the table. "Everyone treats me differently now. Neighbors raise their voices when they talk to me as if losing my sight somehow affected my ability to hear. Girls who barely looked at me in high school are overly sweet when they run into me around town. My mother's friends talk to me like I'm five years old again." Frustration built in Bradley's voice, like he finally had the chance to get everything off his chest and couldn't stop himself. "If I manage something on my own, I either hear, 'How did you do *that without being able to see?' or 'Are you sure you're really blind?'" The joy had drained out of Bradley's face. "Margo's father paid me a visit on Sunday to tell me I ought to do the right thing and let his daughter go." His eyes glistened. "I've applied for a program for the blind in New York that specializes in independent living and skills that'll help me find employment. Even that didn't change his mind."*

Harry wanted to tell Bradley that he understood what it was like to feel like an odd duck. But in his heart, he knew he didn't have a clue what Bradley was going through. Some people treated him differently because of the color of his skin, but at least he didn't carry the burden of being the only Black man in Dennison. He hadn't woken up one day with a different skin color than he had when he went to sleep the night before. The kindest thing he could think of to say was, "People can be peculiar sometimes."

"With some, I don't even have a name anymore. I'm 'that poor blind veteran. What are we going to do with all these wounded men?'"

"But if they see what you did with that lantern, they'll know you're more than that. Margo's father will know."

"I want people to enjoy what I made for its beauty without wondering how a blind man managed to

create such a thing, or me feeling like it's something to help me prove myself. At least for now. So will you promise, and explain to Sylvia and Miss Eileen?"

Harry wanted to argue more with Bradley. Tell him that Sylvia and Miss Eileen would be the first to speak up against anyone who made a "Not bad for a blind artist" remark. But the longer he knew Bradley, and other Dennison men who came back physically or mentally wounded, the more he recognized that it wasn't his place to tell them how to navigate their new lives. He hadn't fought in the war, so he couldn't even say he understood. "Okay, Bradley. I promise."

CHAPTER NINETEEN

$\mathcal{L}$ ater on Monday afternoon, Janet taped one end of the cream-colored vinyl she'd found at the fabric store over a protective layer of taped-down plastic trash bags on her dining room table. Debbie took the other end and rolled it to the opposite side.

Janet slid the roll of masking tape to Debbie's side of the table. "How are we going to catch this person?"

Debbie smoothed down her end of the vinyl. She tore off a strip of tape. "I say we start setting booby traps."

"I'd love to see this town's version of booby traps." Janet looked around for where she'd put the pack of markers from the party store. "I'm picturing water balloons, foam darts, and a slip 'n' slide covered with feathers."

Debbie taped one corner then the other. "Crosby the attack dog snarling at every suspicious person who comes along." She tossed the roll to the center of the table. "Or Laddie. Or both. We need a whole team of dogs."

Janet gazed over at Laddie, sacked out on the floor with a stuffed parrot under his paw. "Oh yes, their faces alone would frighten the most hardened criminal."

Debbie added some tape along the sides of the table. "Did you ever find some large stencils for the lettering on our sign?"

"Tiffany has a set. She's looking for them now." Janet found the pack of paint markers on the dining room chair at the head of the table. She set them on the vinyl.

Debbie smoothed the tape with her fingers and patted the table. "Paulette should be here any minute."

Tiffany ran into the dining room with a large zipper bag in one hand and a plastic cup stuffed with markers in the other. "I found the stencils. I have large letters, plus a smaller set in case you want to label the coffee carafes, and some sheets of swirls and cute shapes." She set the zipper bag on the table then the cup. "I also found these markers in case you need extras. They're acrylic like yours. They still work. I tried them out to be sure. I stuck some pencils in for tracing."

"You saved the day." Janet moved the supplies to the center of the table. "Now we won't fight over the good colors. Do you want to stick around and help with lettering?"

"Sure."

Janet opened the bag of stencils. "But you have to promise not to reveal state secrets to any of the competition. Such as a certain chief of police."

Tiffany pulled out a chair. "What kind of state secrets?"

Janet tried to think up something supersecret. She drew a blank. As soon as Ian caught her with the Salvation Army doughnut recipe, he'd guessed the theme. "I have no idea. But it's fun to say." She wouldn't have been able to keep the details of the café's float secret from Ian much longer anyway. She needed his help securing a table to the base of the flatbed before next Monday.

A knock at the door woke Laddie. He launched into his guard dog impersonation.

"See," Debbie said, "he would be perfect for keeping our float safe."

"Yeah." Janet rushed over and swooped him up. "The perpetrator would do anything to make the noise stop." She snuggled Laddie's head to her chest. "You're so terrifying."

Paulette opened the door and held out a bag to Janet. "I found vintage coffee carafes. One in my garage and the other I borrowed from a lady at church. They look roughed up and everything."

Janet set Laddie down. "Now we have everything we need. I have old serving platters and at least half a pack of lunch sacks right here at home."

Debbie fished the pencils out of Tiffany's markers. "The doughnut bags are arriving Wednesday."

Janet counted doughnuts in her head. "And I have one more batch to make."

Once everyone found places around the table, Debbie took charge. "How about if we take turns tracing letters so we don't trip over each other, then we can all color them in together."

Tiffany volunteered to stencil the first word. She took an elastic out of her pocket and gathered her hair back into a ponytail.

While her daughter traced an *F* and Debbie taped an *R* beside it, a bittersweet wave swept over Janet. Three of the women she loved most in the world fit so beautifully around the table, working together without a tinge of the tension or ego-driven drama that Janet had heard acquaintances complain about when tackling projects with family or certain friends. No matter the results of her application, she wanted to hold this moment as a reminder of why she never felt the need to leave Dennison. She snuck to the kitchen and grabbed her phone to get a picture of Tiffany, Debbie, and Paulette working away.

Tiffany's head shot up. "Are you taking pictures? I didn't shampoo today or put makeup on."

"You look adorable. All of you do. If I'm going to spend three months in a strange city, I'll need lots of pictures of my people."

Once all the letters were traced, Janet got busy with her little band of artists, coloring in THE SALVATION ARMY CANTEEN. FREE SERVICE TO SERVICE MEN.

Paulette pulled the cap off a red pen. "Janet, it was nice of you to stick around to help Ellie today."

"I couldn't feel good about leaving her to make garlands all by herself. It ended up being a lot of fun." She hadn't even felt rushed when she finally left the café. It was one of those moments that she sensed she would treasure while away from her friends at the London School of Cookery.

"Any more leads on who's messing with parade floats?" Tiffany asked.

"None. Even your dad is stumped."

Paulette traced the pencil lines of Tiffany's *F* with red. "The Chamber of Commerce and Event Committee are the only ones who have a list of all the entries."

Janet considered everyone she knew of in those groups. "But no one on the committee has a motive for holding anyone back. They came up with the contest in the first place."

Tiffany reached for a marker. "Maybe it's someone who got left out of the contest when the chamber of commerce cut off entries."

Janet stopped coloring. *The pouty library volunteer.*

Paulette rubbed the thumb of her writing hand. "But the first incident happened before the cutoff."

Janet tried to remember the exact date when Ian told her about the headlights and when Debbie said Greg cut off entries. Ellie would have entered her float and most likely solicited help right away. "Ellie Cartwright said one of her volunteers felt slighted because she chose someone else's artist skills over hers."

"That might motivate her to target the library float, but why the others?" Debbie pointed out. "The variety of groups that had their floats sabotaged seems so random. But my guess is, it isn't."

Paulette went back to coloring. "What would a disgruntled library volunteer have against the police, a construction company, and the Girl Scouts?"

Tiffany's ponytail fell forward. She yanked out the elastic band and started gathering her hair into a bun. "You'd be surprised. People can be so unpredictable when things don't go their way. During junior year of high school, a girl I knew named Brandy got the lead in the theater department's big musical. Another girl who thought the role should've gone to her and ended up in the chorus started pulling pranks on her as revenge. She did infantile stuff like hiding Brandy's script during rehearsal, putting plastic spiders and fake rats in her props, making rude noises when she walked across the stage."

Janet finished the *S* and set her marker aside for a break. "That's terrible." Tiffany had been out of high school for two years, and her stories still left Janet's mind spinning over how cruel kids could be to each other.

Tiffany adjusted her messy bun. "Brandy said the worst part was the girl always resorted to gaslighting. 'It wasn't me,' or 'Your script is right here, Brandy.'"

Paulette stretched her arms. "Did the girl get caught?"

"Yes. On opening night, someone found her trying to rig one of Brandy's costumes. She got kicked out of the show on the spot and barred from future productions."

Debbie dropped a blue marker into the cup and took out a red one. "Serves her right. All that over a part in a high school play."

"Thankfully, Brandy wasn't one to get intimidated easily. She did such an amazing job in her part that the theater teacher recommended her for a summer performing arts camp, and she got a scholarship."

Paulette plucked a marker out of the cup. "The beauty of poetic justice."

"It ended up that half the cast was onto this girl. They just didn't have solid proof until she went too far."

Paulette pulled off the cap. "Which is what will most likely happen to whoever is tampering with the floats."

Tiffany examined her work. "My guess is someone who just wants to win. Like those girls who want to be captain of the dance team so badly that they steal their biggest competition's boyfriend two days before tryouts, so she'll be too devastated to perform well."

Debbie capped her pen and pushed it hard against her palm. "Does your dad realize what a resource he has for solving crimes, right here in his own house?"

Janet got up to stretch. "I can only handle having one member of law enforcement under my roof." A desire to win made the most sense considering the pattern. What better way to take top prize than frustrating other entries?

Debbie pushed her chair back. "The prize is a trophy, not a large sum of money."

Paulette folded her arms across her chest. "And everything was easily fixed."

Janet moved her head to one side and made a slow circle. Two stints with craft supplies in one day had left her tight all over. "But each incident did cause a disruption. Lost time."

Tiffany shot her hand up.

"Yes, dear daughter, do you have something to share with the class?"

"I know some very competitive people at college. Like ridiculously competitive. They don't even need a prize, only the bragging rights of saying, 'I won! I'm Number One!' Or something to put on their résumé."

If only Tiffany's point about bragging rights could get them closer to finding a clear-cut clue that led to their culprit. Janet chose another marker. "I guess all we can do is keep a close eye on our float, watch for suspicious activity, and wait for this person to get sloppy."

CHAPTER TWENTY

An hour after opening the café on Wednesday, Janet squeezed a generous squirt of dish soap into an oatmeal-smeared pot and filled it with hot water. The Hearty & Delicious Oats had been surprisingly popular. She predicted it had more to do with the cups of toppings that came with it than Dennison's citizens suddenly going on a universal diet. Even Patricia had ordered a bowl when she saw that it came with sides of brown sugar, golden raisins, sliced strawberries, and a choice of milk or cream.

Debbie pushed one kitchen door open. "I just sent you a text. I think you'll really like it." She disappeared into the dining room.

Janet turned off the water and checked her phone. She found a screenshot from Debbie of the package tracker for their doughnut bags.

Out for delivery. "Yes." Janet poked her head out. "Why didn't you just tell me?"

"The boys constantly text things to each other while in the same room. I wanted to see what it felt like to be a teenager in the age of smartphones."

"What's the verdict?"

"It was fun, but next time I'll probably use my words."

An alert for a new email caught Janet's eye. She put her phone in her pocket for later but lost her battle with waiting while scrubbing the oatmeal pot.

She let the sponge fall into the soapy water. She tapped her email app.

Sender: The London School of Cookery
Subject: Your recent application

Did she really want to know now, while at work?

She clicked on it. *Yes, I do.* If she got a no, she would find out while within feet of her best friend.

She shut her eyes, tapped the message, and started reading.

> *Dear Janet,*
> *We appreciated the opportunity to review and consider your application…*

She read one more line then gasped and slapped her hand over her mouth at the exact moment when Debbie showed up in the kitchen with a tray of dirty coffee mugs.

Debbie stopped beside the door. "What's going on?" She set her tray beside the sink. "Please don't tell me it's a text from Ian saying another float has been damaged."

Janet shook her head. She let her hand drop and looked over at Debbie. "It's an email from the London School of Cookery."

"And?"

"Glenis wants to interview me."

"When?"

"Three o'clock."

"Janet, that's amazing."

Janet let herself smile. Three o'clock in Ohio would be eight o'clock in London. Glenis must truly be interested if she gave up her evening for an interview. "This might really be happening."

"I need to talk to Paulette about taking on more hours and start interviewing a part-timer."

The jingle of the entrance shifted Janet's attention back to the cafe. She followed Debbie out to the counter to see who had come in.

Jasmine and Amber were at the counter, both in sweatshirts that had seen better days.

"Let me guess where you're headed after this," Debbie said. "Float duty."

Amber eyed the NEW YORK logo on her sweatshirt. "How'd you know?"

Jasmine undid the zipper on a gray hoodie. "I can't believe we're almost done. I'm going to miss Elieen, Ray, and Harry. Harry especially."

Amber reached for a menu. "Jasmine found a new buddy."

"We also found a new approach to research, thanks to the two of you. We're already planning to do some kind of project with our St. Louis focus group next month." Jasmine's face turned thoughtful. She folded her hands in her lap as if wrestling over something. "Janet, thank you for encouraging us to include Harry. It has helped a lot to get to know him after Great-Grandpa passed away."

"I'm glad."

"I feel like I can tell you and Debbie this—" Jasmine looked down at her hands. "A few months before my great-grandfather died, I got in a bad car accident. It affected my vision. Suddenly I couldn't see in color anymore, and it seems to be permanent."

The sadness on Amber's face told Janet that she'd walked closely with Jasmine through her recovery.

Jasmine tucked back her hair. "I thought I would have to give up my dream of becoming a doctor. Research often includes experiments with color differentiation. Even the graphs and charts use color."

Janet thought of the many charts Tiffany created for school projects from middle school to college. "I never considered color as something that could hinder someone. But you're right."

"It was terrible. Besides the frustration of the whole world looking like a black-and-white movie, I felt like I was losing everything I'd worked for." Tears welled up in Jasmine's eyes. "But Great-Grandpa wouldn't let me give up. He told me what it was like for him after losing his sight in the war. Honestly, I'd never thought about that being a major adjustment for him. To me, he was always a member of my family who happened to be legally blind. He started his own business selling train-related metal work. He taught sculpting at a local art school and in programs for kids with disabilities until he was almost eighty. His life motivated me to hold on to my goals. But I went about it the wrong way."

"You were trying to cope with a new situation." Amber spoke gently. "I probably would have done the same thing."

"It was still wrong." Jasmine took a deep breath. "Last semester, I worked as a research assistant on campus, and I tried to get by with keeping my lack of color vision to myself. I thought I could work around it. Instead, it caused me to make an error that would've affected a patient's health had it happened in a clinical setting. Needless to say, I lost the research assistant position."

"I'm sorry." Even though Jasmine didn't come out and say so, Janet sensed that was what she'd been reading when she went from laughing with Amber to looking like she wanted to cry.

"But…" Amber smiled.

"But, when I fell apart over it in front of Eileen, Ray, and Harry and told them what happened, Harry said Great-Grandpa would encourage me to apply for another research position. He would be honest up front and explain how I plan to work around my limitation. So that's what I did."

Amber nudged Jasmine. "Guess who's spending fall semester on an important memory care study at Case Western Reserve?"

"I wouldn't be doing it at all if I hadn't been in Dennison when I got the news about the other job. I'm so thankful for this place."

Debbie went around the counter and gave Jasmine a hug. "We're thankful you came too. The Good Shepherd Retirement Center wouldn't have a float without you and Amber."

Janet was next in line. "You know what? This calls for a celebration. I'm going to the kitchen to make you something gooey and special that has nothing to do with World War II."

Jasmine pulled away from the hug. "Before you go to the kitchen, you want to hear who has a big date on Memorial Day?"

Janet sank into the chair beside Jasmine's. "You?"

"No. I don't have time for dates. Eileen Palmer has a date with Ray Zink."

Amber let out a squeal. "Isn't that cute? He asked her to be his date for Memorial Day."

Janet grabbed Debbie's hands to keep from bouncing out of the chair and jumping up and down like a little kid. Ray had gone above and beyond the movie night plan. "It's the sweetest thing ever. What you girls don't know is, Ray has been secretly in love with Eileen for as long as he's lived at Good Shepherd."

Amber fought to laugh and talk at the same time. "You should've seen Eileen yesterday." She put her hands over her cheeks. "'Girls, what am going to do. I don't have anything to wear on a date.'"

"So," Jasmine said, "Amber and I are taking Eileen shopping this afternoon after we finish decorating."

Janet started walking to the kitchen. "Ray won't know what hit him."

Janet could still smell hints of caramel and chocolate from the brownie sundae she'd made for Jasmine and Amber when she locked herself in the den for her interview with Glenis. Thirty minutes later, she sat at her desk, unable to move from the chair. Glenis had been so down to earth. So easy to talk to. Did the conversation really end as she thought it did?

Laddie's bark and the sound of the front door opening yanked Janet out of a dreamlike state. Janet laid her hands on her laptop. A rush of nervous energy pushed her out of her chair.

She ran her hands over her hair and got up to do who knew what. All the parade supplies were at the depot.

When she reached the hallway, she heard Tiffany bribing Laddie away from her game stash with a treat.

Janet found her daughter in the kitchen tossing Laddie half a dog cookie. "Hey, favorite daughter."

"Hey, favorite mom. How did your interview go? I prayed for you."

"Thanks, honey. It went great."

Janet opened the refrigerator to find something promising to think up for dinner. It didn't feel like another one-pot-meal night.

Why couldn't she bring herself to tell her daughter? Did it matter who she shared the news with first, Ian or Tiffany?

She remembered the Memorial Day task she still had left to do—the batch of doughnuts for Tiffany's cake walk. She went to the pantry for ingredients.

Tiffany cut her off at the door. "Well? What happened? Did you get the job?"

Janet took hold of the knob.

"Mom."

She couldn't hold it in anymore. She had to tell someone, and Ian wouldn't be home for at least two hours.

"I'm one of four candidates."

"Oh." Tiffany tossed the other half a bone to Laddie.

"But she says I have the approachability she's looking for in teachers. She wants a copy of my cookbook. Unofficially, the job is mine."

Tiffany ran over and hugged her. "I knew you'd get it. Why did you leave me in suspense like that?"

"I don't know. Now that I know this is happening, it feels sort of…weird."

At bedtime, Janet sank back against the stack of pillows she'd arranged against the headboard, her mind still processing the notion of spending fall in England. Glenis needed to finalize the decision with her department and send a contract. But everything seemed to be pointing to a fall in London.

God, how did I get here? Aren't I supposed to be solving a float caper right now?

Not that she or Debbie were any closer to finding the answer.

What kind of person were they dealing with? Would petty pranks and disappearing props become more serious in the last couple of days leading up to Memorial Day?

Or during the parade itself?

The buzz of Ian's electric toothbrush signaled the final stage of her husband's nighttime routine. She let out a long sigh and reached for her phone. She knew electronics were a no-no right before bed according to every sleep expert on the planet, but the game of mental ping-pong going on in her head wouldn't help her sleep either. She pushed thoughts of the London School of Cookery aside for later.

Her fingers flew over the mini keypad. *How to catch a vandal.*

Ian came out of the bathroom before Janet could find an article that didn't include a sales pitch for "the best" home security system.

Janet swiped out of her browser and let her phone drop beside her on the bed. Why keep searching the web when she had a real-life crime expert at her beck and call? "Ian, why do people vandalize property?"

Ian pulled back his side of the covers and flopped onto the bed. He kicked off his slippers. "Who knows. Boredom? Anger? Maybe the mindset that they're only playing a joke."

"But why take things off Memorial Day parade floats? It seems so disrespectful. Debbie and I have gone down every possible train of thought. In the end, I can't think of anyone in the community who would have a reason to put a damper on the celebration or anyone's efforts. Everyone I know is excited about the parade and the idea of spending the day playing hokey carnival games while munching on Charla's version of Cracker Jacks."

"What baffles me is that whoever is behind this has gotten away with it four times in two weeks without leaving so much as a footprint behind." Ian reached for a book from his nightstand.

"We have a pretty smart vandal on our hands."

"As frustrating as the situation is, it's nice to see that it isn't stopping people from making this event the best it can be. We haven't seen anyone drop out because of it."

"You're right." Janet moved her phone to her nightstand so she wouldn't end up falling asleep on it. "Every group that's had their float tampered with cleaned up, replaced the item, and moved forward."

"Brendan Vaughn and one of the other deputies think we need to revisit the possibility of senior pranks. The dance team entered a float, and it's now missing a banner."

CHAPTER TWENTY-ONE

ebbie stood wordless beside the sink the next morning. Janet tried to read her response to hearing about the interview.

"Debbie?"

A smile spread slowly across Debbie's lips. She rushed over, arms spread wide, and wrapped Janet in a hug that almost made her cry. "I'm so happy for you."

Janet rested her head on Debbie's shoulder and gave in to a rush of relief. "Don't do dramatic pauses like that. I thought you'd changed your mind about wanting me to go."

Debbie pulled back, still holding Janet's shoulders. "Not at all. I confess, when you said you got the job, it hit me how much I'm going to miss you."

"I'm going to miss you too. I cannot believe this is happening."

"Neither can I. But it really is. We need to celebrate after the parade."

"I feel so strange right now, Debbie. One minute I'm so excited I can hardly breathe, and the next I think I must've been in the throes of temporary insanity to apply in the first place."

"That's because it's new. You've never gone so far from home before."

The very thought made her feel lonely in advance. "Are you sure you don't mind me being gone?"

"I already talked to Paulette and made her pinky promise to let you be the one to spread the news through the entire town. She's all set to play the role of Mini You in the fall, and we're hoping to get Charla part-time. I'll call her as soon as she's finished making mountains of Celebration Caramel Corn."

"What if something big happens while I'm away, like a jewelry theft or the arrival of a tourist who may or may not be who she says she is? I'll miss all the excitement. Though it's possible, based on the many dead ends we've hit with the float situation, that we've lost our touch."

"I promise to chronicle the whole thing and send pictures. And I'm confident we haven't lost our touch. If the police are back to suspecting senior pranks, we can start running down the list of kids who might have an ax to grind."

"What if you find another partner in crime while I'm gone?"

"Impossible. You will always be my partner in crime."

On Thursday evening, Janet re-read the email from Glenis to make sure she wasn't imagining things. *Please find the attached offer letter, contract, and information packet for temporary employees.* "Oh my goodness." She said it under her breath.

She didn't realize how her reaction might sound to her family until Tiffany groaned from the other side of the living room. "Let me guess. Another float is missing parts."

"No, thankfully, this is not about the floats."

"Thank goodness." Tiffany turned the sound back on for a video she was watching on her phone.

Ian came in from the kitchen. "What's going on over there in Janet Land?"

Janet opened the first attachment. It was indeed an offer letter with her name on it, complete with a payment quote, start and end dates for the semester, and a deadline for accepting and signing the contract.

Monday.

"It's officially official." The words came out before she had a chance to think. "I have the contract right here in front of me with the London School of Cookery written in calligraphy with a fancy cake under it."

Tiffany leapt up from the couch. "Woo-hoo!"

"My wife the baking superstar." Ian scooped Janet up and gave her a kiss.

Knowing she would have to wait one quarter of a year for hugs from her husband kept Janet's arms locked around Ian. "Glenis gave me the weekend to accept and sign the contract."

Ian put one arm around Janet and the other around Tiffany and kissed them both on top of the head. "I'll read over the offer and contract tonight to make sure everything looks legit and fair. Then we can start pricing flights to London."

Tiffany went back to the couch. "I am so completely jealous—I mean happy for you, Mom."

Ian plopped down beside Tiffany. "We have a trip with your name on it too. Before your mom got this offer, we'd already started talking about travel, and next summer we're taking a family trip to Scotland."

"Seriously?"

"Seriously."

Janet returned to her chair and the reality of being so far from home. "And Tiffany, if you ever get a chance to do a semester abroad, I am going to have to insist you go."

"Oh, trust me, there will be no insistence necessary."

Janet opened her laptop again and clicked the next document.

Tiffany reclined on the couch then sat up again. "I forgot to tell you. I heard something sad today when Layla and Catherine and I were getting coffee. Eger's Market & Deli is closing."

Remorse for the Egers almost caused Janet to let the computer fall off her lap. "No."

Ian sighed. "I heard that too."

Tiffany did a long, drawn-out exhale. "Goodbye, curry chicken salad. Goodbye, locally pressed and bottled cider. And cheddar chive chips."

Janet looked at her hands over the laptop that held a contract for a new opportunity while Kyle, Renee, and Tristan Eger faced losing their livelihood. "Let's be sure to make a big deal about supporting their float on Monday. I happen to know Tristan is working hard on it."

Tiffany turned her video back on. "I wish we could also guarantee its protection between now and then."

On Friday morning, Janet whipped up honey pecan pie for her Homefront Bakery special. She and Debbie still had a week of retro specials until the end of May, but with the Memorial Day Parade only three days away and signs of celebration already popping up around town, it felt like a day for something extra yummy.

When she went out to put it into the bakery case, she found Harry at the counter with Patricia. "What's this I hear about you moving to London?"

Janet shut the case and sent Debbie a *What happened to pinky promises* look.

"Sorry. It slipped out. I'm just so thrilled for you."

Janet caught the hint of melancholy in Harry's eyes and in Patricia's. "It's only for a semester. To teach a workshop." She did her best to work up a British accent. "At the London School of Cookery."

Patricia straightened up in her stool. "Cookery." She took hold of her mug and stuck out her pinky. "My, my. You're going to come home so sophisticated."

Janet waited for Harry to add something. He stirred his coffee and gazed down at Crosby.

"I'm sure I'll be my same old self but with presents and more recipes. Maybe even enough for another cookbook." Debbie's order sheet for copies had run onto a second page.

Harry finally made eye contact with Janet. "I'm really happy for you, Janet. Even though Crosby and I will miss you a whole lot. It won't be the same around here without you."

She reached out and patted Harry's wrinkled hand. He squeezed hers in return. "I'm going to miss you too."

The feeling of Harry's hand in hers, and the sweetness in his ninety-seven-year-old eyes stayed with Janet all day long. She caught herself fighting a lump in her throat while attaching her end of the Free Service to Service Men sign to the front of the tablecloth on the wooden table that still smelled of paint. Her need to figure out who was trying to sabotage the float competition took a backseat to her desire to enjoy every moment of her part in the parade.

She swallowed. "Ian should be here soon to bolt down the table. Then we can lay out the fake spread of bagged lunches." Every word felt tight coming out of her mouth.

Debbie tapped a nail into her side of the sign. "I'm sorry I told Harry and Patricia about the baking school before you did."

"It's okay." It really was. The whole town would know soon enough anyway. So why did she feel so emotional? "It just made me sad to see Harry sad. It'll feel strange to be away from Harry and Patricia and all the other regulars. To not check in with Ray and Eileen at Good Shepherd. They're like family."

"Three months will go quickly. Before you know it, you'll be back in Dennison and missing your friends in London."

"I can't imagine missing anyone as much as I'll miss all of you." She waved off her sadness. "Oh, I'm just being drippy because everything is official."

She jumped down from the flatbed and used the time before Ian was due to show up to estimate how many stuffed lunch bags she could fit on each tray.

"The café's bakery lady is spreading her wings."

"That's true. I am." Until that moment, she'd never really thought about how much it meant to her to do the baking for the café. To fill her case with cookies, breads, and pies, and watch them disappear. To know what each regular liked best and occasionally be surprised by what sold out. Before Janet had a chance to get melancholy again, Ian arrived with his toolbox and drill.

Ian didn't waste any time getting his drill ready for action. He pointed the bit to the ceiling and flipped the switch. "Out of the way, ladies. Here I come." He turned it off and hopped onto the float platform.

Janet did a mock eye roll, enjoying the way teasing Ian pulled her heart back to the excitement of floats, doughnuts, and her whole community celebrating together. "What is it about men and power tools that turns them into little boys?"

Debbie unfolded a metal chair and sat in it. "Greg is the same way. The other day, I was hanging a collage of wedding photos, and he came over to help, wielding an electric screwdriver and a tray the size of Ohio filled with every variety of wall hanging device in existence. He looked like a ten-year-old who'd been waiting all week for the rain to stop so he could finally ride his new bike."

Janet backed away from the float but kept her eyes on Ian. "Did you remind him you were hanging a picture, not constructing the wall that would hold the picture?"

"I did. He looked—how can I put it? Disappointed." Debbie grabbed her water bottle and took a big swig. "What can I say? He likes building things. His tool cabinet is now known as Greg's Toy Box."

"That drill in Ian's hand is one of three. I've given up on figuring out what makes each one unique and special."

Ian knelt on the wooden surface of the flatbed. "Would this be a good time to discuss the three dozen whisks that have taken over our kitchen? One is as big around as my head."

"Tell you what. We'll call it even." Janet stood beside Debbie. "That whisk is not as big as his head."

Ian activated his drill. He started singing the theme song to a popular children's show featuring talking construction vehicles.

Debbie shouted over the noise, "Drill that bolt in extra tight in case the seniors strike again. We don't have time to find another serving table."

Janet pictured a couple of eighteen-year-olds in trench coats trying to get away while dragging a table bolted to a flatbed trailer and getting stuck in the doorway. "Maybe they'll take our fake lunches, expecting free food. I filled them with rocks and crumpled paper last night."

"Ha!" Debbie snapped the lid on her water bottle. "It would serve them right."

The side door of the garage opened. Debbie and Janet jumped at the same time.

Greg stood in the doorway with an almost unrecognizable Julian.

Debbie checked the time on her phone. "Is it that time already?" She pushed her chair against the wall.

Janet waited for Julian to start looking sulky. "That's right. It's performance night."

Greg put his hands on Julian's shoulders. "He cleans up pretty good, doesn't he?"

While Debbie gathered her things, Janet took in the image of Julian in formal attire, wishing she had her camera within reach. In addition to his button-down shirt, tie, and slacks, Julian had slicked back his hair. Janet detected the scent of a cologne spray that had become popular with the young guys who weren't quite ready for aftershave. She couldn't help noticing Julian didn't appear nearly as reluctant to perform as he did at the beginning of the dreaded dance unit.

"Don't you look handsome?"

"Thank you, Mrs. Shaw."

Debbie hurried to the door with her purse, water bottle, and jacket. "I just need five minutes to change in the café restroom." She waved to Janet. "I'll send pictures."

"You better."

Once the threesome had left, Janet turned her attention to Ian.

He secured the last bolt and sat on his heels. "Anything else I can bolt into place, so it doesn't get taken between now and Monday?"

The Saturday before Memorial Day brought an extended current of holiday weekend traffic at the café. Janet barely had more than a few minutes together to chat with Debbie. She savored every busy moment of cooking, baking, and keeping up with breakfast and lunch orders as something she would most likely pine for come September. She stayed after closing and used the quiet time to double check her supply of frozen parade doughnuts. Tiffany's dozen was set aside at home, so she could add icing and sprinkles early Monday morning and present them to her daughter in a bow-topped box.

Debbie flew into the kitchen. "Float decoration time. Paulette will meet us in the garage."

Janet did a final doughnut count. Thanks to opting for mini ones she had well over a hundred. She shut the freezer. "First, I want to hear all about the performance."

Debbie leaned against the counter nearest the sink. She released a breathy chuckle. "How can I describe last night? Other than it was the one of the most awkward, adorable, refreshing displays I've ever witnessed."

"I still have pictures from Tiffany's. Every boy looked like he was taking the worst final ever."

"Julian actually did a great job. They invited the parents to join a dance party at the end."

"That's right! They make it a surprise. Did you and Greg go up?"

"Of course we did." Debbie put her hand on her heart. "And Julian got the award for Most Improved Dancer. It was my first proud mom moment."

"After all that angst." Janet changed from her apron to a sweatshirt with a row of dancing cupcakes across the chest. "When Greg picked you up, I didn't see any signs that Julian had to be dragged from the house kicking and screaming either. Did he discover a new passion for ballroom dance?"

"No. His assigned dance partner for the show happened to be a girl he's had a crush on since sixth grade."

"That explains the change in attitude."

"And the stylish hair. And the cologne."

Janet pushed her way through the double doors. "It's not too late to add him and his dance partner to our float. We can be behind the table with Paulette while they frolic along the sides and pass out doughnuts."

"I don't think he enjoyed it *that* much." Debbie held open the café door. "After you."

When they arrived at the shed, Paulette ran over pulling a wagon. "Here I am. Do you like my creative caddy?" The wagon held all the serving trays and coffee carafes they'd collected over the past three and a half weeks.

Janet took hold of the handle. "I need one of those."

Paulette plucked a roll out of the wagon. "I brought double-sided tape for securing the trays and lunch bags."

Debbie unlocked the shed and flipped on the light. She stood rigid in the doorway. "Oh boy." She turned around. "Ladies. It's our turn." She stepped aside and waved her arm toward the float.

It took Janet a moment to figure out what Debbie was talking about. The float looked fine.

Paulette parked her wagon against the wall.

Then Janet's eyes shot back to the front of the canteen table that Ian had secured to the flatbed the previous night. "Where's our sign?" The edge of the table lay as bare as before Janet and Debbie nailed in the sign with a tack hammer. "I locked the door last night." Her gaze drifted to the pull-up garage door at the front of the old repair room. They hadn't opened it since parking the flatbed, so she'd never thought to check the latch.

Debbie sank into a metal folding chair against the wall. "We can't remake it. The fabric store closed at two and isn't open on Sundays."

Paulette tossed aside her roll of tape and walked over to the front of the float. "This is getting kind of disturbing." She gestured to the roll-up door. "You'd never know anyone but us had been in here."

Janet went over to the rolling door to check for any signs of damage to the latch. "If we really are dealing with seniors, they're so not getting free cookies on graduation day."

Debbie rested her elbows on her knees and her chin in her hands. "Other than you telling Ian, playing investigator won't help us now. We need to figure out what to do about our sign."

Paulette stood and paced in front of the float. She pulled her phone out of her pocket. "I've gotten proficient at using those free design apps for photo books and Christmas cards, and I have some heavy-duty paper at home. How about if I create something on the app while the two of you tape down the platters and coffeepots. Then I can print it when I get home. I'll have to tape the pages together, and it won't be nearly as nice as the one we made at Janet's, but at least we'll have a sign."

Janet pictured the sign she, Tiffany, and her friends worked so hard on flung over the edge of a dumpster behind Dennison High School. She allowed herself one giant pout. "Sounds like a plan."

She went to the wagon and picked up the roll of double-sided tape. "Thank You, Lord, for technology."

CHAPTER TWENTY-TWO

Dennison, Ohio
May 24, 1946

Right after school on the Friday before Memorial Day,
Sylvia raced home to change into her new work dress
for her first training session as a receptionist. She left
plenty of time to stop at the depot to say hello to Harry.
On her way into the station, she straightened her crisp
gray skirt. Her brown wedges felt stiff on her feet, but
oh so professional.

She found Harry beside the route map and train
schedule. He looked at her in a way he never had
before.

Sylvia smoothed the hair that she'd done her best
to arrange into a neat bun. "Do I look okay? Is my hair
coming apart?"

"*You look great. I'm just not used to seeing you in a bun.*"

"*I'm not used to it either. Mama insisted this job called for one.*"

Miss Eileen came into the waiting area with something big in her hands, covered with a blue velveteen blanket. "*Well, don't you look nice for your first day of work?*"

"*Thank you, Miss Eileen. I'm just training for an hour or so.*"

"*Do you have time to take a peek at what I found outside my office this morning? I think you'll both like what you see.*"

Sylvia checked the clock over the ticket booth. She still had thirty minutes until her training.

Miss Eileen went to a little table near the ticket booth and set down her bundle. Sylvia followed Harry over. Miss Eileen lifted the velveteen cover and revealed a lantern that looked so unlike anything Sylvia typically saw around the station that she sucked in her breath.

Miss Eileen laid the cover aside. "*I knew the two of you felt confident that Bradley could create something nice for the float, but I never expected this.*"

Harry said, "*Neither did I. He let me see it the other day, but since then, he's added swirly etches to the base and top.*"

Sylvia took a step closer to admire Bradley's work. If he were entering a contest like in high school, the lantern would take top prize for sure. "And you haven't even added the ribbons and flowers yet."

Eileen took an envelope out of her blazer pocket. "He left a note." She handed it to Harry. The expression she exchanged with him indicated she'd read it already.

Sylvia noticed all three of their names on the envelope. "That's Margo's handwriting. I recognize it from when she dropped off the flowers."

Harry pulled a folded sheet of paper out of the envelope and started reading.

Sylvia tried to guess the contents. "What does it say?"

Harry's eyes bore a hint of confusion, like Bradley's words had thrown him for a loop. "It says, 'Dear Harry, Sylvia, and Eileen, thank you for giving me the honor of making this lantern for the Dennison Depot float. I can't express what it has meant to me to create art again. I'm sorry I couldn't give the lantern to you in person and participate in the parade as planned. The school for the blind I told Harry about had a last-minute opening for summer term and a scholarship to go with it. By the time you read this, my folks and I will be on the road to New York. I want you to know that the Dennison Depot will always be a place I remember fondly for giving me my confidence back as an artist and as a man. Yours, Bradley.'"

Sylvia tried to digest what she'd just heard. "Bradley is gone."

"I'm happy for him." Harry returned the note to Miss Eileen. "He needs a fresh start. He told me so."

"I'm happy for him too," Sylvia said. "But what about Margo?"

Bradley's note, mingled with excitement for the parade and the flood of instructions she got during receptionist training, kept Sylvia's mind busy all weekend long. When she wasn't quizzing herself on the correct way to answer the phone at her new job, she imagined Margo crying over Bradley leaving for New York, most likely because they'd both buckled under the pressure to break things off.

She spent the night before the parade tossing and turning. She finally threw back her covers at a little after five in the morning and declared an early start to Memorial Day. She put on some clothes, brushed her teeth, and went to the kitchen, where her mother was already at the table with a cup of coffee.

"I'm going to put some finishing touches on the float." It seemed like the only way to escape her spinning mind. She grabbed a carrot for her breakfast and gave her mother a kiss on the cheek.

The station was quiet when she arrived on the property. She stopped at the garbage can on the platform to toss the end of her carrot. A pretty young woman walked out of the depot carrying a suitcase in one gloved hand and a pink handbag in the other.

Sylvia almost didn't recognize Margo in an ordinary dress, coat, hat, and pumps. She had a ticket between her fingers and a look on her face like a little girl running away from home. Sylvia met her at the bench. "Good morning, Margo. Where are you headed so early? You're going to miss the celebration."

Margo opened her purse. She straightened her shoulders. "I'm going to New York." Her voice sounded shaky. She set her suitcase beside the bench and deposited the ticket into her purse.

Sylvia looked into Margo's blue eyes. "I know about Bradley leaving. I'm so sorry."

Margo did a quick glance around the platform. "I'm not. Not at all." She hung her purse over her arm. "I'm going to meet him in New York."

"I thought he was going to school. He said his folks were driving him there."

"He is. They did." Margo checked her watch then the tracks. "We worked everything out. I'm staying with a high school friend who is recommending me for a job at a hospital near the school for the blind. On his first free day, we're getting married."

"You're eloping?"

"Shh. Yes. I'll have to keep living with my friend until Bradley finishes the program. Then we'll find a place of our own."

"What about RN school?"

"I'll find a way to pay for it myself. I'm doing what you said. I'm sticking with the man I love."

But I didn't think you would— A train whistle blew. The eastbound train would make a brief stop when it arrived, so Margo still had a few minutes. "Are you sure? Your parents will be worried sick."

"I left them a note. By the time they read it, I'll be on the train and gone. As soon as Mother tells her friends the news of how I disgraced the family by running off to marry Bradley, the whole town will know within hours."

The eastbound train pulled to a stop.

Sylvia wanted to beg Margo to think about what she was doing. But the determination on Margo's face silenced her. Sylvia reached out to give Margo a hug goodbye. She could feel Margo's love for Bradley in the tightness of Margo's embrace. "You take care of your-self, okay. Write to me as soon as you can."

"I will." Margo squeezed her hand. "You're a good friend, Sylvia."

Before Sylvia could say anything else, Margo let go of her hand, picked up her suitcase, and rushed to the train.

It was all Sylvia could do to focus on the float. Each time she heard a noise, she expected Margo's parents to storm over to her and demand to know who to contact to stop the train, as if that were possible. As soon as Harry arrived at the garage they'd used to transform Mr. Palmer's old Ford into a train car, Sylvia poured out her encounter with Margo and how worried she felt for her, even in her happiness over the thought of Margo and Bradley being together.

"When I told her to stay true to the man she loves, I didn't expect her to hop a train for New York." Margo was plenty old enough to manage a train trip alone, but New York was a big city. What if her friend didn't meet her as planned? What if the job recommendation didn't work out? "This is my fault."

Harry guided Sylvia to sit on a chair against the wall. "You didn't do anything wrong. They've obviously been planning this for a while if they sorted out the details as soon as Bradley heard from the school in New York."

Sylvia's heart suddenly hurt for Margo's parents. Until she reminded herself that they were the ones who drove their daughter away. "Maybe they both need a fresh start."

"I think they're going to be okay, Sylvia. When I saw what Bradley made for us, I knew he'd be able to find work eventually. He just needs God to send him someone who sees his talent more than his blindness."

Sylvia moved off the chair and over to the float. Clusters of Margo's paper flowers hung under each window, tied with fat bows. Bradley's lantern sat waiting on a table, decorated with tissue-paper poppies and red, white, and blue ribbons.

Miss Eileen knocked on the shed door. In each hand, she held the folded tops of three of the biggest striped bags from the candy store. "Harry, would you like to put one of these at each veteran's place in the truck?"

Harry went over and took the bags off her hands. "I'll do it right now."

Miss Eileen came over to the table where Sylvia still stood staring at Bradley's lantern. She fingered one of the paper roses. "After the parade, we should display this in the depot. It's too beautiful to put away."

Sylvia picked up the strands of soft satin ribbons. She let them fall through her fingertips. "It's too bad the town won't know who made our focal point, as Bradley called it."

"Who knows? Maybe someday they will."

CHAPTER TWENTY-THREE

*A*s much as Janet needed to be home defrosting doughnuts or at the depot putting last-minute flourishes on the float, skipping church was out of the question for her the day before Memorial Day. She had a contract to sign and an ache in the pit of her stomach that refused to budge.

What's wrong with me, Lord? I wanted this. Everyone is happy for me. Debbie, Paulette, Ian, Tiffany, even her parents. They saw she had a great opportunity and shouldn't pass it up. *I want to do this, God. Help me to stop second-guessing myself. I know that's what I'm doing.* The homebody in her simply didn't want to step out in faith and do something new. *What am I afraid of, Lord? That I'll miss everyone too much?*

Miss Ian.

And Debbie.

Seeing Harry and Patricia every day?

Seeing what grew out of Ray and Eileen's date.

Everyone will still be here when I get back.

Ian and Debbie would be a video chat away. Plus she would have full days of teaching to keep her busy. *The three months will probably feel more like three weeks.*

Pastor Nick's sermon became more like white noise than an impactful message as Janet prayed and mulled over what lay ahead.

An adventure.

A chance to teach in a storybook-like location, send postcards that required international stamps, and come home with recipes to share, travel stories to tell.

Updates to hear about all she'd missed.

A lot could happen in three months. For her and her friends at home.

After church, Janet put her seesawing thoughts aside. She laid out sandwich fixings for a quick lunch before she, Ian, and Tiffany went in their own directions for the final day of parade prep.

Tiffany rolled together slices of ham and cheese and laid them on a paper towel. "See you at the station. I'm picking up my costume then need to set up games."

Janet waved her daughter off just in time for Ian to swallow a bite of his turkey and cheese sandwich and tell her, "I'll see you there too. I told Harry I'd drive his float over to the station so it's ready to go when we all head to the start of the parade route tomorrow. Amber and Jasmine are tied up with something today." He gave Janet a kiss on the cheek. "I read your contract. Everything looks good."

Janet's stomach did a little jump. "I guess I can send it then." She topped her sandwich with a slice of sourdough. "After Debbie and I finish up our float."

Thirty minutes later, she was on the platform in front of the depot watching volunteers wrap lamp posts with red, white, and blue bows, counting off the community events she would miss between mid-September and mid-December. Tiffany ran up the steps with a garment bag slung over her shoulder. "Costume. Check." She let the bag slide over her arm and down in front of her. She unzipped the front. "Tada!"

Janet saw the poofy red-and-white striped skirt and couldn't restrain herself. "Go into the restroom and model it for me."

"Since you're leaving soon and I can tell you feel unsettled about it, I'll cater to you."

"What makes you think I feel unsettled?"

"I can just tell. You've being very reflective today."

Janet felt her eyes start to mist over. Her heart wanted to tell Tiffany how right she was, but her voice refused to cooperate. So she pulled her daughter into a hug. "I can't wait to see it."

Janet followed Tiffany into the station and watched her disappear into the women's restroom. The door opened behind Janet.

"Hey, honey." It was Ian. "Have you seen a costume around here?"

She saw her husband standing in the doorway with Harry. "Tiffany is getting ready to model hers right now."

"This one's a dog costume." Harry looked as if he were ten years old again and searching for a lost toy. "It's for Crosby, for the parade. I had it here yesterday when I stopped in for lunch. The bag also had a new leash and some dog food in it. When I finally had a chance to take everything out last night, the costume was gone. I wondered if it might've fallen out."

"I haven't seen anything like that." Janet scanned the benches in the waiting area and peeked through the café window. "Maybe it dropped outside. I'll help you look."

Janet rapped on the restroom door. "Meet us outside, Tiffany. We need to help Harry with something."

"Okay."

Outside, Janet saw Charla coming from the parking area pushing an old-fashioned popcorn maker.

Janet called to her, "Did you happen to see a dog costume on the ground in the parking lot?"

Charla carefully lowered the front end of the popper. "No. But I can help you look as soon as I get this over to the snack bar area."

Janet looked under the benches along the wall of the depot. Harry checked the trash bin. "I hope I didn't leave it behind in the store. They special ordered it for me."

Ian stood at the railing looking out over the activity of table and awning setup. "Harry, did you leave the bag unattended at all yesterday?"

"I might have turned my back on it to talk to folks in the café. I was careful not to take the costume out though. I wanted it to be a surprise."

"It was a costume for the parade, I assume."

"Yes."

Janet watched her husband's expression change from questioning friend to chief of police who might be onto something. His remark connecting the costume to the parade turned a light bulb on inside Janet's brain. "Do you recall who was around you at the café?"

"It was really busy when I stopped by. The last people I talked to were some girls from the high school."

Ian turned his back to the railing. "Which girls?"

"They were from the dance team, buying cinnamon rolls and coffee before heading to one of their houses to make a new banner to replace the one that was taken."

Janet considered the likelihood of girls who'd had their banner stolen turning around and robbing an old man of his dog's costume.

Debbie came up the stairs at the other end of the platform. "What am I missing out on?"

Janet watched dejection build on Harry's face. Where could they find another dog costume? "Crosby's parade costume went missing."

Debbie dropped her tote bag on the first bench she reached. "Who is taking these things? The Invisible Man?"

Tiffany came out of the depot dressed in her poofy skirt. It looked even better on, with a blue star-spangled vest, a white blouse, and a black glittery top hat. "Well? What do you think? Tomorrow I'll be wearing red tights and cuter shoes, but you get the idea." She did a little twirl. "Layla's and Catherine's outfits are similar but with striped pants instead of the skirt, and a different hat."

Janet slapped both hands over her cheeks. "That is precious."

Tiffany adjusted the hat. "I might put my hair in tight rollers to make wild curls." She shifted her attention to Harry. "Why do you look sad, Harry?"

Janet searched the area over the railing hoping to see a dog costume. "Take a guess. It involves parade preparation."

Tiffany yanked off her hat. "This thief has sunk to a new level of low."

Charla's voice cut Janet off from any sort of response. "Janet, Ian. Can you come in here, please?"

Janet followed Ian's bold strides toward the alcove where Charla's snack bar was set up in the depot. Debbie, Harry, and Tiffany trailed behind her.

Ian took a step into the alcove. He poked his head out. "Hey, Janet, Debbie, Harry, you'll want to see this."

As soon as Janet reached the door, she saw the FREE SERVICE FOR SERVICE MEN sign that she, Tiffany, Debbie, and Paulette spent hours creating at her dining room table. Someone had folded it over the top of a plastic bin, under the worktable where volunteers once wrapped sandwiches, sliced sheet cakes, and filled paper sack lunches. She picked it up and popped open the bin.

Behind her, Harry shouted, "Crosby's costume!"

There at the top of a pile of items lay a dog vest designed to resemble striped train engineer overalls and a cap with ear holes cut out of it. She handed them back to Harry. "Tiffany, you now have the second cutest costume."

Crosby followed Harry outside, wagging his tail and panting.

"I know, boy," Harry said. "I'm excited too."

Janet retrieved a rolled-up plastic banner that she guessed belonged to the dance team and pushed the bin to Ian. "I found your headlights."

Ian rescued them from the bin.

Debbie took a peek. She pulled out a white garbage bag and untied the drawstring. "And what do you know? A big bag of red poppy garlands."

Tiffany scooted closer. "Is there anything else?"

Janet checked the bin one more time. A metal sign fell from the side to the bottom with a whoosh. SAVE SCRAPS FOR VICTORY! METALS, PAPER, RUBBER, RAGS. She took it out and held it up. "I'm assuming the thief saved this as a souvenir after taking down Troop 1096's scrap drive pyramid."

Ian held one headlight in each hand. "The only thing missing is evidence of dumped potting soil."

Charla tapped her fingernails on the popcorn maker. "You want to know the strangest part? That bin wasn't in here when Patricia and I came by yesterday to drop off supplies, or at six thirty this morning when I brought over a case of hot dog buns." Charla pursed her ruby red lips. "I locked the door last night but forgot to after dropping off this morning's load. I remembered during church and sent up a prayer for the Lord to protect the snack supply."

Janet hung the sign over her arm. "People have been coming and going all day to set things up. I doubt anyone would consider a person walking into the depot with a plastic bin suspicious."

Charla pushed the popcorn marker to the spot where the plastic bin had been. "Whatever happened, we have everything back now and a lot of work to do for tomorrow."

Debbie retied the bag of poppies. "Tiffany, since Ellie's daughter is on your team, do you want to take this to the Cartwright's?"

"I'll text Catherine now to tell her it was found." Tiffany started walking toward the box car already marked MIDWAY with a long banner. She stopped. "What if this person strikes again during the event tomorrow?"

Ian patted her shoulder. "They will be doing it at a public event that includes a float full of law enforcement members."

"Maybe we'll finally catch them then."

CHAPTER TWENTY-FOUR

Janet attached the last scallop of streamer to the edge of the flat-bed. After backing up to admire the portable Salvation Army Canteen, she put her arm around Debbie. "We did it."

Debbie rubbed Janet's shoulder. "The sign looks so beautiful."

Ian stepped onto the flatbed. He gave the table a jiggle. "I think it's as secure as it's ever going to be. All you need to do is hitch it to the truck tomorrow."

His phone went off. "Hang on a sec." He pulled his phone from his front pocket. "Hello, this is Ian."

Janet took a moment to double check her and Debbie's time slot for picking up helium balloons from the party store.

"Is everything all right?" Ian asked.

Janet tried to read her husband's expression. She looked at Debbie and shrugged.

"Sure," Ian said. "Janet and I are at the depot. Debbie is here too. Come on over. We're working on a float in one of the sheds, so text me when you get here." He ended the call and returned his phone to his pocket. "That was Kyle Eger. He asked to talk to us. He sounded upset."

Janet picked up the last of the patriotic streamer roll. "Upset as in mad or upset like something bad happened?"

"Kind of a combination."

Janet remembered Tristan's excitement over creating a float for the parade. "You don't think their float got vandalized."

"We'll find out."

Ian's phone dinged ten minutes later. He typed a short reply. "I'm going to meet him outside."

Ian had barely stepped outside when Janet heard him shout, "Over here, Kyle. What's up?"

"Can we chat with you guys?"

Janet glanced over at Debbie. *We?*

"Of course." Ian came back inside and made way for Kyle.

Renee was behind him, along with Tristan. Even from the flatbed, Janet could see Tristan had been crying. Tristan hesitated at the door. Kyle called him over, his eyes filled with a sea of emotions that Janet couldn't pinpoint.

Tristan dragged himself forward.

Kyle stood behind him, one hand gripping each of his son's slim shoulders. "Tristan has something to tell you."

Tristan avoided eye contact with everyone in the room.

So did Renee. But it didn't prevent Janet from recognizing the pain in her face.

"Dad," Tristan said under his breath, his eyes desperate. "Let me just tell Officer Shaw. Please?"

Kyle ushered his son forward. "You might as well tell Mrs. Shaw and Mrs. Connor at the same time."

Tristan rubbed his hands over the legs of his sweats. His downcast eyes never left the ground. "I took the stuff from the floats." Tristan's voice cracked, making his confession especially pitiful.

Renee looked like she wanted to run from the scene before she gave her son another tongue-lashing in front of everyone. "We don't know what he was thinking. I am so sorry."

Kyle kept his hand on his son. "I saw him tiptoeing down the hall this morning with a big bin and something flopped over it. I figured he was going to work on the float in the backyard and didn't want to wake us up. Until I went out back and he wasn't there."

While Kyle and Renee poured out their humiliating tale of Tristan's sneaky return and attempt to jump back into bed, Tristan's eyes grew tearful.

"After I took Crosby's costume, I felt terrible for what I did. I wanted to return everything, but I didn't know where to start. So I figured someone would find the bin in the depot."

Janet waited for Ian to go into investigator mode. Instead, he put one hand on Kyle's arm and whispered something to him. He wrapped an arm around Tristan, walked him over to the float and invited him to sit.

He sat beside Tristan. "I heard you had a soccer game the night Greg Connor's float was vandalized. How'd you manage to be in two places at once?"

"Two of my friends from school helped me. But it was my idea."

"You want to tell me why you messed with the floats in the first place?"

Tristan sniffed hard.

Ian turned his head. "Hey, Janet, can you find us some tissues, please?"

"Sure." Janet hopped off the float and rummaged through her tote bag for a half-full packet of tissues. She went over and handed the pack to Tristan. She patted his shoulder. "It's okay. You can tell us. You don't seem like a kid with a criminal record, so I assume you had a reason for what happened."

"I did it because…" Tristan swept the tissue across his eyes. "Because I wanted our float to win so our store wouldn't have to close, and Dad wouldn't be depressed anymore."

Janet thought back to the day Tristan begged his father to enter the contest. "Because a winning float would draw customers."

"Yeah."

Ian leaned forward with his elbows on his knees. "So you figured undoing work on other floats would set people behind?"

Tristan nodded and blew his nose. "My friends and I picked floats we heard about at school or at the library. I know it was dumb. I kept hearing Mom and Dad talking about losing everything and got scared."

Kyle crouched in front of Tristan. "Tris, winning a contest isn't going to save the store at this point."

Janet's eyes met Renee's. "So you're really closing?"

"The ceiling collapse uncovered other structural issues."

Kyle got to his feet. "As we tried to explain to Tristan a couple weeks ago, the building was old when we took over the lease. Some of the damage isn't covered by insurance, and our deductible for the rest is high. We can't afford the repairs. I've gotten three quotes, and they're all more than we can manage. Closing is the only option unless we want to go broke."

"Are you going to arrest me now?" Tristan's eyes were so red and swollen that he almost appeared sick.

Ian squeezed Tristan's shoulder. "No. I'll have to file a report and talk to the other boys involved. But you confessed. Everyone got their items back undamaged. I don't expect those affected to file charges." He stepped away and shook a finger at Tristan. "But don't ever forget the feeling of thinking you might be arrested."

"I haven't been able to sleep all week. I've felt so bad."

Kyle eyed his son. "In addition to being grounded from everything except school and eighth grade graduation, Tristan agreed that the right thing to do would be to pull out of the float competition."

Janet wanted to beg Kyle and Renee to stay in the contest. Tristan couldn't be more distraught over what he'd done. They were losing so much. Missing out on the biggest community event of the year would only isolate them when they needed friends most. But as a parent, she would have done the same thing with Tiffany.

Tristan looked down at his shoes, clearly spent from all the crying and confessing.

Ian went over to Kyle. "I hope you'll still come to the celebration. You're part of the community."

Tristan gave his nose another noisy blow. "You guys can go tomorrow. I'll stay home and take apart the float." He balled up his wad of tissue. "I'll feel worse than I already do if you stay home."

"We'll see." Kyle gestured to Tristan to stand up. "We better go. We have a few more people to talk to."

Tristan slid off the side of the float. He walked over the Janet and looked up at her like a sad puppy. "I really am sorry."

"I know you are." Janet reached out and gave him a hug. "We forgive you. I'm sure everyone else you apologize to will say the same thing. Everyone in town knows you're a good kid."

"Thank you."

Debbie reached her arms out to him. "Come here. We all still love you."

Janet saw that Renee looked about to lose it and gave her a hug too.

"Thank you for being so kind." Renee put her arm around her son. "You have no idea what the past few weeks have been like. Your response reminded me why we love living in Dennison so much."

Janet waited for the Egers to leave before she let the reality of what had just happened set in. "I didn't think it was possible for me to feel so sorry for a boy who upset the entire community."

The streamer spool rolled off the float bed. Debbie grabbed it. "The ones I feel the sorriest for are Kyle and Renee. Having to deal with what their son did while also losing their business."

"When it rains it pours is an understatement." Ian placed one foot on the float. "There must be something they can do to avoid closing their doors. File Chapter Eleven bankruptcy or something. Though I'm sure they considered that option."

Debbie rewound the streamer. She tapped it against her thigh. "I think I know of a solution."

Tiffany took a break from sorting prizes into buckets on the living room floor. "How sad. He thought you were going to arrest him?" She tore open a bag of plastic kazoos. "I may regret getting these."

Janet moved to the floor and took a handful of kazoos. "Remember when you were in kindergarten and knocked over a salad dressing display in the grocery store?"

"That is exactly what I thought about just now."

"When I heard the crash and you let out a wail, I thought one of the bottles broke and cut you. But no, you thought you were heading straight to prison for breaking something in a store."

Tiffany dropped a green kazoo into one of her buckets. "I pictured myself being carted away in handcuffs and having my mug shot taken in one of those striped jumpsuits."

Janet slam-dunked a bright pink kazoo. "I think that's what Tristan was picturing today. He could not stop crying."

"Aw. Did you cry too? I would have."

"Almost. The whole scene was so pathetic."

Ian put his hands up. "Come. On. I feel for him too, but let's not forget, unlike the famous salad dressing episode, Tristan had a legitimate reason to fear consequences. Technically, he did trespass and steal. Small items, mind you, but people aren't always as forgiving as we were." Ian reached for a bag of mini stuffed animals and took out a bunch. "If he didn't live in a town like Dennison where everyone knows him and his family, he could have been in more trouble than having his parents ground him and pull his float from the parade."

"I'm glad you forgave him. Everyone has their float decorations back, and Tristan didn't end up in the dungeon." Tiffany leaned against the couch and set aside the kazoos. "It's too bad about the Egers' store. It's not their fault the roof caved in."

Janet took a stuffed dragon out of the bag. She adjusted its wings. She thought about her cookbook. The profits would make a nice donation, but they couldn't save the store. "Debbie's talking to Greg about an idea that she hopes might help them."

Tiffany opened a bag of heart-shaped sunglasses and sorted in silence for a while. She bit her lip. Janet sensed something brewing in her daughter's mind. Before she could ask, Tiffany blurted out, "What about applying for grants? Small businesses can send proposals for funding to cover repairs, safety upgrades, all sorts of things."

Ian dropped a mini beagle puppy into a bucket. "I would never have thought of that."

"Is the application process hard?" Janet found a home for the dragon in the red bucket.

"There's a format and an art to writing proposals. And you have to know how to find the right donors. But I could do it for them."

"You could?"

Ian tossed another animal into a bucket. "When did you learn how to write grant proposals?"

"Last semester. The business class I took covered grant writing. We had to write one as a final project." Tiffany picked up a pair of pink glasses and dropped them into another bucket. She crumpled the empty bag and tossed it aside.

Ian reached for a bag of yo-yos. "Since you're so smart, would you like to drive the truck for the café float tomorrow?"

Janet blushed. In all the excitement, she and Debbie had failed to consider who would drive their creation down the parade route.

"Yeah, I would."

Janet watched Tiffany go from explaining grant proposals to sorting more prizes as if helping possibly save a business was no big deal at all. Could it actually work?

CHAPTER TWENTY-FIVE

*A*fter all Tiffany's prizes were sorted, Janet stole away to the den and reread the contract one more time. Then again.

What's the deal? Sign it already. She could almost hear a cheer section made up of Debbie, Mandy, Tiffany, and Ian. *"Sign, sign, sign, sign! Go, Janet. Go, Janet."*

She clicked through the months on the calendar app in the bottom right corner of her computer. By the time she came home from three months in London, Tristan's desperate attempt to win the float competition would be stowed in Dennison's memory banks with a hundred other stories, unburied secrets, and solved crimes.

Friends like Harry, Eileen, and Ray would be older. One of them could possibly even…

She chased away the thought.

She checked the time on her phone to make sure she didn't ruminate her way into the wee hours. Her home screen lit up with a text from Debbie.

GIVE ME A CALL. GREG AND I CAME UP WITH A PLAN TO HELP KYLE AND RENEE.

She replied with a thumbs-up.

God, I can't imagine three months without my friends.

Maybe she would discover friends in England who were just as quick to rally around a family in need. Drop everything for a crisis. Get to the bottom of a family mystery that emerged out of nowhere.

But it still wouldn't be the same as spending every day in the town she grew up in.

Being surrounded by people whose first gut reaction to a need was to figure out how to help.

Who didn't consider any crisis too small or silly—not even lost float props—or too inconvenient or hard.

She tapped her phone app to call Debbie with the computer curser still blinking on her contract's signature line.

On Memorial Day, Janet tucked a stray lock of hair into the victory curl Paulette had spent so much time spraying into place. Helium balloons bobbed in the wind on either side of the tableful of taped-down lunch bags and coffee carafes. Her heart felt lighter since talking to Debbie. *Lord, thank You for showing me why I felt so conflicted.*

Debbie handed Janet a tray of bagged doughnuts. "I hope the Egers come today," she said to Paulette. "I can't wait to tell them about Greg's offer. Janet and I also want to do something through the café."

Paulette played with the skirt on her polka-dot dress. "This is just an idea, but what if you create a support fund for local businesses that customers can contribute to? They can round up their bill to the nearest dollar, drop spare change into a bucket, make a donation as a group, whatever they want to do. Stores do it for other things. Last week, I rounded up a grocery bill for a garden project for underprivileged kids."

"Funny you should mention that." Janet chose a scarf from the bag of thrift store purchases and swung it over the back of her neck to see how it looked against the gingham apron with baked goods pockets. "I want to use the profits from my cookbook to start just such an account. Debbie and I researched the setup process last night. Once Eger's Market opens again, we can let the fund grow for the next need that comes up."

Someone tapped Janet's shoulder. She turned around and saw Amber dressed in a vintage stationmaster's uniform.

"Don't you look cute?"

Amber spun around. "It's Eileen's old uniform. Kim let me borrow it from the museum because I'm driving the float today. It was her idea." She touched Janet's arm then Debbie's. "Follow me. Harry wants you to see something before the parade starts."

Janet handed her tray over to Paulette. Her sensible nineteen-forties loafers slapped on the ground as she hurried to keep up with Amber's eager strides.

Debbie called from behind, "I need to start working on my cardio."

Amber stopped in front of a float that looked almost exactly like the one in the photograph from Memorial Day 1946. Ray sat in his wheelchair beside a ramp at the back of the float, wearing his army uniform. Harry was clad in his smart navy blue coat with two rows of brass buttons and the matching billed hat he'd worn for years as a conductor. Crosby matched him, and didn't even seem bothered by the hat. Eileen had on a uniform that resembled what she'd worn as stationmaster, but it fit her older frame. Eileen shuffled over to Janet and whispered in her ear, "The girls picked out something much more stylish for me to change into after the parade."

Harry tugged on his jacket. "In a perfect scenario, I would've worn my porter uniform from during the war. But the ole body has changed a bit since then."

Janet's words caught in her throat. She felt as if she'd been pulled back to 1946 with her precious friends.

Jasmine came around the side of the truck holding a station-master's lantern decorated with ribbons and artificial flowers. She had on an army hat that a male soldier would have worn during World War II.

Janet wanted to reach out and touch the flowing ribbons. "Is that the same one from your original float?"

Harry came over, looking so handsome in his conductor's uniform. "It sure is. My old friend Brandley Macomb—Jasmine's great-grandfather—made it."

"Where in the world did you find it?"

Jasmine ran her fingers through the ribbons and gently smoothed them. "It was at my parents' house. My mom found it among Great-Grandpa's things after he passed. She liked it, so Great-Grandma Margo said she could have it. I saw it in a picture that my parents sent, told them about Harry, and they gave it to me for the float. Amber and I went to get it over the weekend and decorated it like the original."

"So Bradley had it all this time?"

Debbie came over for a closer look.

Eileen raised her hand. "I'm the guilty party. I sent it to Bradley and Margo a week before I married Rafe. While emptying my desk at the station, I saw it on a trolley of things destined for storage. The new stationmaster thought the lantern had had its day. So I asked if I could take it. I thought it would be nice to send it to Margo and Bradley. They'd eloped, you see, and were living in New York. Margo had sent me her new address, so I mailed them the lantern as a reminder that they would always have friends in Dennison who loved and believed in them."

"I'd been promoted to on-board porter by then," Harry interjected. "So I had no idea."

Jasmine handed the lantern to Eileen. "Now, just like in 1946, Eileen will carry the lantern. This time, instead of a welcome home, it will be to honor every man and woman in Dennison who came through or left from this station."

"I'm sitting in the passenger seat though." Eileen took the lantern in both hands with the same care her daughter took with historical artifacts. "My marching up front days are over, I'm afraid."

Janet was about to offer her hand to help Eileen get into the truck when Greg rushed over. "Time to get back to your float. The parade's about to start."

CHAPTER TWENTY-SIX

anet handed out doughnuts as fast as she could grab them off
the tray, fill outstretched hands, and trade an empty tray for a
full one. The high school marching band's tune sounded familiar—
she'd heard it at least ten times in the café in the past four weeks—
"My Dreams Are Getting Better All the Time." She sang along in
her head.

Mandy waved to her from the sidelines.

"You came." Janet held out a doughnut.

Mandy grabbed it just in time. "I wouldn't miss this."

All of Dennison seemed to move to the beat of Dennison High
School's horns and drums, alive with the beautiful heartbeat of the
community's history and tight bond.

God, did I do the right thing?

Out of the corner of her eye, she saw ribbons from Eileen's lantern blowing from the window of the float right behind the café's
makeshift canteen.

Peace filled Janet's spirit.

Yes. I know I made the right choice.

The parade ended at the depot. Tiffany parked in the spot designated for the Whistle Stop Café float. She hopped out of the cab,
already in her game operator costume.

"How's that for parallel parking?"

Janet savored the sight of her daughter high-fiving Layla and Catherine, her hair a wild mass of red curls under the black top hat.

"Okay," Tiffany instructed her friends. "Let's go play some games."

Janet opened the passenger side of the pickup to stash her empty tray on the seat.

"Oh, Janet." Patricia's singsong voice came from the other side of the passenger door. "I have a surprise for you."

Janet shut the door and saw Patricia standing with her hands behind her back. She looked delightful in her pin-striped apron and paper hat. A far cry from her usual slacks, cardigans, and blouses.

"Pick a hand."

Without stopping to overanalyze, Janet tapped Patricia's right arm. "That one."

Patricia held out a bag full of caramel corn speckled with Spanish peanuts. "Charla made this bag especially for you."

"Lucky," Debbie whined over her shoulder.

"You better get some," Patricia told Debbie. "It's going fast."

Janet plunged her fingers into the bag. She popped a perfect cluster of popcorn and peanuts into her mouth. "Mmm." *Lord, I love having friends who make caramel corn.*

"Now, check your prize."

Janet dug to the bottom, doing everything possible to avoid losing half the caramel corn.

Debbie grabbed a handful. "Let me help you out."

Finally, Janet's fingers connected with a flat wax paper pouch. She pulled it through the mountain of popcorn until it surfaced in her sticky fingers. She glanced at Patricia.

Patricia raised her eyebrows.

Janet took out a little card. She flipped it over and saw a layer cake with angel wings. A plastic sheet covered the image. Janet laughed so loud and hard that passersby started giggling too. "A temporary tattoo!"

"As soon as we saw it this morning, we knew it had your name on it." Patricia gave her a hug. "Enjoy."

"Tell Charla I will treasure it forever."

She held the bag out to Debbie. "I will never find friends like this again."

"No. You will not." Debbie took a pinch of caramel corn and tossed it into her mouth.

Janet saw Mandy coming toward her. She had her doughnut bag in one hand and a half-eaten Salvation Army doughnut in the other.

Debbie patted Janet's arm. "I'll let you visit. I should find Greg so we can talk to Kyle and Renee."

Janet put the tattoo in the pocket of her dress.

Mandy took a bite of her doughnut and covered her mouth to finish chewing. When she finally swallowed, she said, "You have got to teach doughnut making at the London School. Did you sign the contract? Glenis is thrilled to have you."

Janet shook her head. She pulled Mandy aside to an area with fewer people. "Mandy, I am so grateful to you for recommending me to Glenis. When she invited me to teach—I can't even call it a dream come true because it wasn't something I ever thought to dream of. But last night when I was about to sign the contract, I just couldn't."

"What's stopping you?" Mandy slid the last bite of doughnut into its bag. "You were so sure."

"I know I was. Until I wasn't." Janet watched Jasmine offer Eileen her arm and accompany her into the depot and knew Eileen was about to change into her date outfit. "I realized I don't want to be away from all these people for so long. At least not right now."

Mandy's mouth parted like she was about to argue, then closed into a gentle smile. "I understand. I really do. I won't pretend I'm not disappointed."

"And I won't pretend this was an easy decision. But I know it's the right one." Janet saw Ray Zink beside the depot float watching Eileen with Jasmine. "The London School of Cookery and opportunities like it will always be out there if I want them, but I can't say the same for friends like Harry and Ray and Eileen. I want all the time I can have with them."

Mandy rolled her eyes upward like she was trying not to cry.

"Maybe I needed to know I could do it." Janet took Mandy's hand. "I'm sorry."

"I'm not getting emotional because of your answer. I promise you, I'm not. As much as I wanted you as my roommate and a buddy to run around London with, I also knew from the start you would be leaving a lot behind." Mandy looked around at the crowd. "If I had friends like yours, I wouldn't want to stay away for three months either. I envy what you have here. Your friendships. The sweet people who come into your café. Running a restaurant with your best friend. I have the freedom to teach in England for three months because I don't have much keeping me at home anymore." Mandy took Janet's other hand and squeezed both of them. "So if you ever catch yourself thinking less of your life because you've stuck close to home, know there is at least one person out there wishing she could live in your world for a while."

Janet let go of Mandy's hands so she could give her a hug. "You are welcome in my little world any time."

"I look forward to taking you up on that."

CHAPTER TWENTY-SEVEN

anet found Ian with Debbie and Greg in Charla's concessions line. Before she could decide if she wanted a corn dog or regular hot dog, she spotted Renee and Kyle.

"Renee," she shouted. She whispered to Debbie, "Here's our chance."

Janet whisked Ian out of the line and caught up with Renee and Kyle near Tiffany's game car. "I am so glad you came." She waited for Greg and Debbie to weave their way through the crowd.

Kyle gazed in the direction of the floats lined up near the depot. "We felt bad leaving Tristan home to take apart his float. But he insisted, and Renee and I decided it would be good to give him space to think. His, um, assistants are on restriction as well."

Debbie took Greg by the hand. "Kyle, Greg and I came up with a way to help you."

"That's nice of you, but I don't think—"

Greg held up his hand to interrupt. "I'd like to offer my construction services at cost to repair your roof."

"Like we told everyone yesterday, there are other issues besides the roof."

"Debbie told me that part. I'd like to check those out for myself and repair them at cost too."

Renee watched her husband with a *Please, do not pass this up* longing her eyes.

Janet took advantage of the pause in the conversation. "Tiffany offered her services as well, to write some proposals for small business grants."

"What?" A light that had gone out of Kyle Eger's face rekindled before Janet's eyes.

Debbie slipped her arm through Janet's. "But wait. There's more."

Janet released her nervous energy into gripping Debbie's wrist. "We've decided to use my cookbook sales to start a small business support fund at the café. It'll take a while to grow it, but if the grants don't work out, or you end up with some financial gaps, your store is first on our list."

Renee watched Janet as if waiting for the catch. "After what Tristan did, you're still willing to help us?"

"Of course." The words came out of Janet's mouth without so much as a pause. "We don't want to lose Eger's. You're as important to Dennison as our café."

"I—Thank you." Kyle fumbled over his words. Janet saw on his face that he was fighting emotion. "I'm tempted to go home right now and tell Tristan."

Greg shook Kyle's hand. "I'll call you tomorrow so we can set up a time for me to look at your roof."

The screech of a microphone drew Janet's attention to the depot platform.

"Ladies and gentlemen." Kim stepped away from a big monitor near the platform steps. "It's time to announce the winner of our float competition."

Janet moved closer to Ian. She rubbed her thumb and index finger together. "Get ready to hand over that extra spending money."

Ian whispered back. "I've had at least three people tell me the police department's float was the best they've ever seen."

"We'll see."

Kim took a clipboard from the table behind her. "First I want to thank our history teachers from Dennison High School for serving as our panel of judges." She put on her reading glasses. "All the entries were so excellent that it's a shame we can't give a prize to everyone. But the Event Committee did decide to acknowledge second and third place in addition to the winner. So without further ado, third place goes to the Claymont Library for their beautiful tribute to Dennison men and women who lost their lives in World War II."

Ellie Cartwright went to the front and waved to the crowd.

"And in second place, we have the Whistle Stop Café for recapturing the Salvation Army Canteen, complete with doughnuts." Janet tried to mask her disappointment over losing out on extra money in Scotland. She hurried to the front with Debbie and took her place beside Ellie.

"And now for the top prize. The trophy for first place goes to Good Shepherd Retirement Center for their salute to Dennison Station." Kim took the trophy from the judges' table and held it up high. "I wish I had a special award for Crosby for that outfit."

Amber pushed Ray Zink's wheelchair forward. Eileen walked alongside, wearing a spring floral dress. Ray's eyes remained glued to her for the entire walk to the platform. Harry took up the rear with Jasmine on his arm.

Debbie whispered to Janet, "They are so getting married."

"Now I'm glad we didn't win."

Janet and Debbie took turns throwing their arms around Harry, Eileen, Ray, Harry, and the two young women who made Harry's dream float happen.

Kim presented the trophy to Harry. He raised it like a football champ who'd finally won the big game.

Harry leaned into the mic. "We have our friends Jasmine Green and Amber Wells to thank for our float." He said something in Jasmine's ear. She nodded and left the platform.

Amber sneaked around Harry to Kim, who handed over the microphone.

"So, for the past few weeks, my friend Jasmine and I have been researching longevity in the elderly. Janet Shaw was good enough to encourage us to let go of our rather sterile approach and get to know Harry, Ray, and Eileen while assisting them with their float. I thought you'd all enjoy knowing some of our findings. Because what we discovered has as much to do with you as it does Harry's, Ray's, and Eileen's obvious zest for life, healthy lifestyles, and positive outlook. One thing Jasmine and I noticed immediately was the friendships they have through Good Shepherd Retirement Center and the Whistle Stop Café. This whole town really. If we had to name one thing that sets them apart, it's their strong, loving community."

Janet leaned toward Debbie's ear. "That's exactly what I hoped they'd discover."

"Me too."

Janet saw Jasmine trying to discreetly get back to the platform and find a spot while holding her great-grandfather's lantern in both hands.

"Come on over here, Jasmine." Amber made room for Jasmine. "When I'm a hundred years old, I want to live in a town like Dennison." She handed Jasmine the microphone.

Jasmine motioned for Harry to stand next to her. "Harry, how about if you start our story?"

Harry took the mic with one hand and put the other hand on Jasmine's shoulder. "You might recognize this lantern from an article in the *Gazette*. Back in 1946, Dennison celebrated the one-year anniversary of the end of World War II on Memorial Day right here at the depot." He moved his hand to the top of the lantern. Janet noticed his hand trembling a bit. "Eileen Palmer, my late wife Sylvia, and I designed a float like the one you saw in the parade today with the help of a young veteran named Bradley Macomb. Bradley was an artist and sculptor who'd lost his eyesight while fighting in the Pacific. We commissioned him for a special piece for our float, and this is what he made." Harry took the lantern from Jasmine and held the handle with the same pride as when he'd accepted the first-place trophy. "Back then, Bradley asked us to keep his identity anonymous, for fear people might dwell more on his being blind than on the piece itself. Jasmine and I agreed that Bradley would be okay with us giving him credit today. I'll let her take over from here."

Harry gave Jasmine the mic.

Jasmine did a quick sweep under her eye with her fingers.

Amber gave her a sweet side hug.

Jasmine took the lantern from Harry. Its stream of ribbons rippled in the afternoon breeze. "Bradley Macomb was my great-grandfather. He passed away on April first of this year at ninety-eight after a long life that included starting his own business, raising a family, and teaching sculpting. One thing I will always remember is his stories about living in Dennison. During a difficult time in my life, he told me he'd found his purpose here when he thought he'd lost it forever. He didn't get a chance to share the details, but I heard them through Harry and Eileen. It turned out my mother had the lantern that all of you thought was missing. I want to present the town of Dennison with this stationmaster lantern. The first piece made by the sculptor behind a company known as Macomb's Railway Crafts."

Harry started the applause. Janet saw tears escape his big brown eyes.

Janet waited for Harry to call Kim over and present the lantern to the depot museum. She could see it in a display of its own, complete with the flowers and red, white, and blue ribbons.

Harry took the microphone from Jasmine. "Janet, Debbie, would you come up here, please?"

Janet exchanged dumbfounded looks with Debbie. She walked up the steps with her best friend at her side. She positioned herself between Debbie and Harry. In the crowd, she spotted Mandy, standing with Patricia and Charla. Her parents were with Tiffany.

Harry held out the stationmaster's lantern. Light caught the etchings in the panels around the lamp. "Debbie and Janet, in the two years since you opened the Whistle Stop Café, Dennison has found a gathering place for good food, friendship, and occasionally finding answers to unexpected questions."

Janet grabbed Debbie's hand. The good food she'd expected to serve, but the friendships and mysteries had come as exciting surprises.

Debbie warned, "Janet, don't you dare cry, or I will too."

A ripple of laughter crescendoed through the crowd.

Ray took hold of Eileen's hand, and Harry held the lantern out to Debbie. "We couldn't think of a better location for this than in a café like yours that has filled Dennison with light."

Debbie took the lantern and drew Janet close with her other arm. "The Whistle Stop Café wouldn't be what it is without my friend Janet."

Janet felt a wave of feelings from her feet to her heart that she wouldn't have been able to explain if asked to. All she knew was, nothing—no prestigious baking school or chance to expand her world beyond Dennison, Ohio—would ever compare to what she had with Debbie at the café. "It wouldn't be what it was without every person who comes in for breakfast and lunch and their morning coffee."

Debbie gave the lantern a graceful twirl. "You know what, Janet? I think we should hang this right outside the entrance as a welcome to everyone who comes to the café."

Harry started another round of applause. "I think Bradley would approve."

Kim thanked parade participants one more time, and the crowed started to disperse. Janet saw that one of the lantern's red ribbons had caught in an artificial rose. She freed it with her fingers and watched it fall in line with the rest. "For me, this will be a daily reminder of why I plan to grow old right here in Dennison."

Whatever God had waiting for her in the future, she would always come back to where she felt most at home.

Harry looked down at Crosby. He did a double take. "Crosby, what's that on your vest?"

Janet followed Harry's gaze. Sure enough, there was an envelope tucked under the straps of Crosby's engineer overalls.

Debbie rescued it. She read the front, turned it over, and flipped it over again. "It has your name on it, Harry."

"Where did this come from?" Harry took the envelope from Debbie.

Janet checked behind her and out into the clusters of friends breaking off toward Charla's concessions and Tiffany's game car. "I was so into Jasmine's speech that I didn't see anyone else come up."

Debbie pointed out, "Whoever delivered it has gorgeous penmanship." She handed it back.

Janet glanced over at Debbie. A rush of excitement awakened her to the prospect of finding the answer. "It never ends. Just when one mystery gets solved, another one takes its place."

"Let's face it," Debbie said. "Our lives wouldn't be complete without the intrigue."

Dear Reader,

I thoroughly enjoyed writing this last installment of the Whistle Stop Café Mysteries series. I will miss hanging out in the café with Janet, Debbie, Harry, and Crosby.

One of the things that draws me to write for series like this one is being part of a team of authors that brings a story world to life. We work as a group, but each of us has a unique voice and experiences that drive our tales. For *My Dreams Are Getting Better*, I created characters who share my challenges of living with limited sight (I have been legally blind and without color vision since birth) and overcome the social hurdles that come with any kind of disability. Like me, they gained confidence to step beyond expectations with the support of friends.

For this final book in the series, I also wanted to celebrate the tight-knit community that Janet and Debbie are part of. I pray that Janet's journey will deepen your appreciation for the good people God has placed in your life, whether you've stayed close to home or found family all over the world.

Happy Reading!
Jeanette

ABOUT the AUTHOR

*J*eanette Hanscome is the author of a dozen books, including fiction and nonfiction. She is a regular contributor to Guideposts' *All God's Creatures* devotional and enjoys serving on the board for West Coast Christian Writers.

Trains are Jeanette's favorite mode of transportation, whether taking a quick jaunt to visit a friend or riding through the Irish countryside.

When she isn't writing, Jeanette gravitates toward all things creative, especially now that her two sons are grown. Being born with a rare visual impairment, congenital achromatopsia, has not stopped her from dabbling in art, knitting and crocheting, and performing. After decades of singing, she took up ukulele during the pandemic with the help of YouTube videos. Experimenting with a variety of styles, including classical music on baritone uke, is one of her favorite ways to relax after a day of writing. Jeanette writes and creates from her home in the San Francisco Bay Area.

A GLIMPSE of the PAST

*D*uring and after World War II, the United States faced the challenge of helping the many injured soldiers in need of rehabilitation. This included thousands who had been blinded or had their sight impaired in battle (or because of poor conditions in POW camps). A large number were blinded in both eyes, while more often they were left partially sighted, or had vision in only one eye.

The government relied on residential schools for the blind where veterans could learn Braille, get vocational training in fields like woodworking and electronics, and gain skills that allowed them to live independently. Around 200 men got rehabilitation at the New York Institute for Special Education, where in addition to the tools mentioned above, they learned adaptive versions of basketball, baseball, and other sports. The school even had a large victory garden during the war.

In 1945, a group of veterans who had lost their sight and were recovering together at the Army Hospital in Connecticut founded the Blinded Veterans Association (BVA). Thanks to their efforts, and gaining support from the VA, the first Blind Residential Center exclusively for veterans opened on July 4, 1948. BVA now has thirteen residential centers across the country and fifty-two regional groups that help veterans connect to services they need. The blind and visually impaired community also benefitted from post-World War II advancements in Orientation and Mobility training. I imagine that Bradley Macomb would have even encouraged his fellow veterans' creativity.

FROM the HOME-FRONT KITCHEN

Celebration Caramel Corn

Charla Whipple's Cracker Jacks-inspired caramel corn was a big hit at the Dennison Memorial Day Celebration. The good news is this delicious peanut popcorn is easy to make.

This recipe makes a lot, so if you want a smaller batch, you can easily cut the ingredients in half.

Ingredients:

10–11 cups popped popcorn

2 cups lightly salted Spanish peanuts

1 cup packed brown sugar

¼ cup corn syrup (light or brown depending on your preference)

1 stick butter

¼ teaspoon salt

½ teaspoon baking soda

½ teaspoon vanilla

Directions:

Preheat oven to 250 degrees F.

Toss popcorn and peanuts in a large bowl and/or pan. Place in the oven to keep warm.

Melt butter in a saucepan over medium heat. Stir in the sugar, corn syrup, and salt. Bring to a rolling boil, stirring constantly. Boil, covered, without stirring for 5 minutes (watch the heat to make sure the syrup doesn't burn). Remove from heat and stir in baking soda and vanilla.

Immediately pour liquid over the warm popcorn and toss until well coated.

Spread in a shallow baking pan or roasting pan. Bake for 45 minutes, stirring every 15 minutes.

Remove from the oven and transfer popcorn mixture to a foil-covered surface to cool. Store in an airtight container.

If you want to take it up a notch:
If you are making your popcorn for a party, neighborhood picnic, or book club gathering, borrow Charla's idea and serve the snack in individual bags with a small surprise at the bottom of each one, reminiscent of Cracker Jack. Inexpensive, individually wrapped prizes such as temporary tattoos, stickers, elastic rings, and beaded bracelets are easily found online or in the party aisle.

Read on for a sneak peek of the first book in an exciting new series
from Guideposts Books—Mysteries of Blackberry Valley!

WHERE THERE'S SMOKE

BY LAURA BRADFORD

*E*arth to Hannah. Come in, Hannah."

Startled, Hannah Prentiss set down the cleaning cloth and raised her head to find her best friend, Lacy Minyard, watching her closely. "I'm sorry. Did I miss something?"

Lacy nodded to the long folding table erected in the middle of the yard. "Nope. Everything looks absolutely amazing. The sandwiches. The salad. Your special peach lemonade, and those *cookies*! Are you trying to fatten us all up?"

Hannah gestured toward the hustle and bustle that was their church group. "Everyone is working so hard to get this place cleaned up for Miriam that it only seemed right to give them a proper thank-you meal. It's easy enough when you own a restaurant."

Closing the gap between them with two long strides, Lacy commandeered the cloth from Hannah's hand. "Hold still. You've got a smudge of soot on your cheek." She gave it a quick rub. "And now you don't."

"Thanks."

"Of course. I suspect you'll do the same for me at some point before we call it quits for the day."

Hannah took the cloth from Lacy and tossed it into the bag at her feet. "Every time I walk through Miriam's front door, I praise God that she was at her son's place in Cave City when the fire broke out. If she hadn't been…" She stopped, drew in a breath, and held up her hands. "Miriam is fine. That's all that matters. And the house—well, we're making progress, right?"

"We are." Lacy hooked her thumb in the direction of the yard. "Are we ready to call everyone to the table?"

Hannah took a mental inventory of every place setting, every food platter, every waiting cup. When she was satisfied all was ready, she nodded to her friend.

Soon, after hands were washed and a blessing shared over the meal, a dozen members of their church women's group pulled folding chairs up to the table and began to eat, the exhaustion from the morning's work blanketing them in a rare silence. Occasionally, a pocket of conversation sprang up, but it didn't last long against the pull of the food as they worked to refuel their bodies.

"Hannah, this salad is amazing," said Connie Sanchez, the church secretary.

The round of nodding that accompanied Connie's words continued as Vera Bowman commented on the deliciousness of the sandwiches as well.

"If you haven't found your way to her restaurant yet, I can assure you that this"—Lacy motioned toward the food around them—" is just a preview of what the Hot Spot has to offer."

More nods made their way around the table until Vera cleared her throat and took the conversational baton again. "I have to say, I was a little skeptical about a restaurant coming into the old firehouse, but you made it work, Hannah," she said. "My kids love your food, and I like knowing they're eating things that were grown and raised in and around Blackberry Valley."

"Thank you."

"I imagine you've had quite a lot of culture shock though," Connie said, eyeing Hannah across the top of her lemonade.

Hannah set her cup down. "You mean after working in Los Angeles?" At Connie's answering nod, she continued. "I mean, sure, LA and Blackberry Valley are very, *very* different. And the restaurants I worked in there were more high-end than the Hot Spot is, but high-end doesn't mean better, and I wanted to come home. To Blackberry Valley. Back to Kentucky."

"And I'm so glad you did," Lacy said, resting her hand on Hannah's and giving it a squeeze. "Having you back in Kentucky these last few months has been such a blessing."

"For me too." Returning her friend's smile, Hannah pushed away from the table. "God led me home at exactly the right time."

The sound of tires against gravel stole her attention to the driveway and the navy blue sedan slowly making its way toward the one-story home. A glance into the passenger seat showed the reason they were all there.

"Miriam's here," Hannah said. She, Lacy, and a handful of others rose to their feet. "I was hoping we'd have everything done before she came."

"Miriam Spencer may be lovable, but she's also as stubborn as the day is long," Connie said. "She's no more capable of staying away than her son is of telling her no."

It was hard not to smile at the accuracy of Connie's words. It was even harder not to smile when Miriam opened the door and got out before her son could make his way around the car.

"Goodness, how long have you all been here?" Miriam asked, her sharp gaze darting from the women walking toward her, to the table, and then to her beloved home of nearly sixty years.

Connie stepped forward. "We got here shortly after sunrise."

"Sunrise?" Miriam shot an accusatory glare at her son, Tom. "Why didn't you wake me and bring me over sooner?"

"Because you need your sleep." Hannah sidled up beside the eighty-five-year-old and planted a kiss on her wrinkled cheek. "And we wanted to surprise you by getting everything cleaned up before you returned."

Leaning against the open car door, Miriam pointed the end of her cane first at the house and then the women. "It's *my* house that caught on fire."

"Yes, but Ecclesiastes chapter four, verse nine, says two are better than one because together they can work more effectively," Hannah reminded her. She gestured at the women assembled around them. "So we came, twelve strong. We plan to get right back to work after lunch."

Miriam lowered her chin and eyed Hannah over the top of her glasses. "And who's running your new restaurant while you're here?"

"I closed for the day."

"You closed a new restaurant for an entire day?" Miriam repeated, drawing back.

"Yes, but that's okay. Tuesdays tend to be slow anyway."

"And your staff is okay missing a day's pay?"

"I'm still paying them."

"You haven't been open long enough to be giving paid days off," Miriam scolded.

"It's one day, and I'll make it work. Being here, doing this, is more important. Truly."

Rolling her eyes, Miriam turned her attention to Connie. "And who's at the church office right now?"

Connie patted her pocket. "I've forwarded all calls to my cell."

"And you?" Miriam shifted her focus to Lacy. "Who's looking after those chickens of yours?"

Lacy swapped grins with Hannah. "My chickens are fine, Miriam."

"We *want* to be here," Vera said, and the others echoed agreement. "To help get you back into your house."

"Helping me is fine. Doing it without me isn't." Miriam planted the end of her cane on the ground and shoved her car door closed. "So, let's get to it, shall we?"

The group made its way back to the house, stopping en route to pick up the cleaning supplies and brooms they'd left beside the front door at lunchtime. Connie and her group of five broke right toward the kitchen, Vera and her helpers made a beeline for the primary bedroom, and Hannah and Lacy led Miriam and Tom into the living room.

"We've made a lot of headway on the smell in here, and we've pulled up the floorboards closest to the fireplace, as you can see." Hannah crossed the remaining scorched floorboards and retrieved the pry bar she'd left in the corner. "If we can get the rest of these up by the end of the day, the men can come in and put in a new floor on Saturday."

Miriam gazed around the room, tsking softly beneath her breath.

"It's all fixable," Hannah said soothingly. "Even the guest room with all of its damage. Really. And you're safe and sound. That's all that matters."

"That's what I keep telling her," Tom chimed in.

"I don't know if I have the strength to pull up floorboards," Miriam murmured.

"You don't have to. Lacy and I have this covered. Right, Lacy?"

"Right." Lacy pointed at the stack of books they'd made that morning. "But if you could inspect those and rid them of any soot, Miriam, that would be helpful."

Miriam's gaze skirted to the books. "I can do that."

"Perfect."

When the elderly woman was settled in a folding chair on the other side of the room, Hannah, Lacy, and Tom got to the business of pulling up floorboards. Board by board, they made their way from the fireplace to the center of the room, setting some aside and discarding others out in the yard.

It was slow, tedious work as they stood, crouched, and stood, again and again as the June sun made its way across the sky, trading the noon hour for the afternoon, and then the afternoon for the early evening.

Rolling her shoulders in an attempt to work out a growing kink, Hannah took a moment to survey what was left and weigh it against the chores she knew still faced Lacy at her farm. An hour's work, maybe, if they continued the course. Two hours if she took over from this point by herself.

"Lacy?"

Her friend wiped a bead of sweat from her face. "What's up?"

"Go home. I'll take it from here."

"I can't do that," Lacy protested.

"You still have farm chores to take care of. Go."

Lacy pulled her phone from her back pocket and consulted the screen. "Are you sure? Because I could do those and come right back."

"I've got it. Really."

Lacy put her pry bar down and stood. "I'll clean up from lunch before I leave."

"Vera already took care of that," Tom said from the corner of the room where he was working.

"See?" Hannah waved toward the door. "All that's left are the horses."

"The horses and that corner of the room," Lacy said, pointing at the section behind Hannah.

"I've got it," Hannah repeated, smiling. "We can finish up."

In an effort to prove her words, Hannah crouched down, worked the hook of the pry bar between the board she'd most recently dislodged and the loose one beside it, and pulled. Her gaze fell on a small wooden compartment cast in shadows. "Whoa. What's this?" she said as she leaned closer.

"What's what?" Lacy and Tom asked in unison.

She reached inside and ran her fingers along the intact wooden box. "It looks like a hiding place of some kind."

The thump of Miriam's cane was followed by her voice from the other side of Hannah. "A hiding place?"

"Yes, look." Pointing to the box, Hannah glanced at her elderly friend. "You don't know about this?"

"No. And I've lived here for nearly sixty years. Tom?"

"I had no idea."

Hannah handed him her pry bar and addressed Miriam again. "The lid isn't on right—it's crooked. Do you want me to look inside?"

"I think you'd better."

Hannah pushed aside the compartment's lid and reached inside the dusty box, her fingertips grazing paper before landing on something round and hard and—

She closed her hand around the object and drew it out. When the object was revealed, they all gasped.

"Whoa," Hannah murmured at the sight of an exquisite ruby brooch, its large gem sparkling in the early evening rays slanting in from the open window.

"It's magnificent," Miriam said in a raspy voice.

Tom squatted down beside Hannah. "I don't understand. How could something like this be hidden under a floorboard in a home my mom has owned for longer than I've been alive—yet none of us knew it was here?"

Hannah heard the question, even registered it on some level, but her focus was on the brooch. A brooch that sparkled in the sun.

"I don't know how I *couldn't* know," Miriam said, shaking her head. "It's my house. Before now, I would have said I knew everything about this place."

"You never had a reason to pull up the floor, Mom," Tom pointed out.

Hannah looked from the polished jewel in her hand to the dusty box in which it had been hidden, her gaze landing on the other item she'd felt. Tom reached inside and pulled it out. "Is that a piece of newspaper?" she asked.

"I think so." Holding it to the side temporarily, he blew dust off the paper. "Put there as a cushion to protect the brooch, I'd guess."

Hannah watched Tom carefully smooth out the page to reveal a torn advertisement for what appeared to be classic cars and then returned her full attention to the ruby brooch as she rose to her feet. "I wonder how long this has been here."

"Based on the dust and the fact that Mom's lived here for almost sixty years, I'd say a long time." Tom balled up the piece of newspaper and tossed it in a nearby trash can. "A *very* long time."

"If you're right, and this was here before Miriam moved in, someone has come back to it since," Hannah said.

Miriam eyed Hannah. "How can you know that, dear?"

Hannah held out her hand and opened her fingers to reveal the brooch. "Look at it. Look at the way it shines."

Miriam gasped again. "You're right. It's been freshly polished!"

A NOTE FROM the EDITORS

We hope you enjoyed another exciting volume in the Whistle Stop Café Mysteries series, published by Guideposts. For over seventy-five years, Guideposts, a nonprofit organization, has been driven by a vision of a world filled with hope. We aspire to be the voice of a trusted friend, a friend who makes you feel more hopeful and connected.

By making a purchase from Guideposts, you join our community in touching millions of lives, inspiring them to believe that all things are possible through faith, hope, and prayer. Your continued support allows us to provide uplifting resources to those in need. Whether through our communities, websites, apps, or publications, we inspire our audiences, bring them together, and comfort, uplift, entertain, and guide them. Visit us at guideposts.org to learn more.

We would love to hear from you. Write us at Guideposts, P.O. Box 5815, Harlan, Iowa 51593 or call us at (800) 932-2145. Did you love *My Dreams Are Getting Better*? Leave a review for this product on guideposts.org/shop. Your feedback helps others in our community find relevant products.

Find inspiration, find faith, find Guideposts.

Shop our best sellers and favorites at
guideposts.org/shop

Or scan the QR code to go directly to our Shop

If you loved Whistle Stop Café Mysteries, check out this Guideposts mystery series!

SECRETS FROM GRANDMA'S ATTIC

Life is recorded not only in decades or years, but in events and memories that form the fabric of our being. Follow Tracy Doyle, Amy Allen, and Robin Davisson, the granddaughters of the recently deceased centenarian, Pearl Allen, as they explore the treasures found in the attic of Grandma Pearl's Victorian home, nestled near the banks of the Mississippi in Canton, Missouri. Not only do Pearl's descendants uncover a long-buried mystery at every attic exploration, they also discover their grandmother's legacy of deep, abiding faith, which has shaped and guided their family through the years. These uncovered Secrets from Grandma's Attic reveal stories of faith, redemption, and second chances that capture your heart long after you turn the last page.

History Lost and Found
The Art of Deception
Testament to a Patriot
Buttoned Up
Pearl of Great Price

Hidden Riches

Movers and Shakers

The Eye of the Cat

Refined by Fire

The Prince and the Popper

Something Shady

Duel Threat

A Royal Tea

The Heart of a Hero

Fractured Beauty

A Shadowy Past

In Its Time

Nothing Gold Can Stay

The Cameo Clue

Veiled Intentions

Turn Back the Dial

A Marathon of Kindness

A Thief in the Night

Coming Home

Find more inspiring stories in these best-loved Guideposts fiction series!

Mysteries of Lancaster County

Follow the Classen sisters as they unravel clues and uncover hidden secrets in Mysteries of Lancaster County. As you get to know these women and their friends, you'll see how God brings each of them together for a fresh start in life.

Secrets of Wayfarers Inn

Retired schoolteachers find themselves owners of an old warehouse-turned-inn that is filled with hidden passages, buried secrets, and stunning surprises that will set them on a course to puzzling mysteries from the Underground Railroad.

Tearoom Mysteries Series

Mix one stately Victorian home, a charming lakeside town in Maine, and two adventurous cousins with a passion for tea and hospitality. Add a large scoop of intriguing mystery, and sprinkle generously with faith, family, and friends, and you have the recipe for *Tearoom Mysteries*.

Ordinary Women of the Bible

Richly imagined stories—based on facts from the Bible—have all the plot twists and suspense of a great mystery, while bringing you fascinating insights on what it was like to be a woman living in the ancient world.

To learn more about these books, visit Guideposts.org/Shop